MW00509630

Empathy
at
Scale

PUBLICOVER

PRESS

EST. 2016

First published by Publicover Press 2020.
Copyright © 2020 by Dana Publicover.

All rights reserved. No part of this publication may be reproduced, stored or transmitted in any form or by any means, electronic, mechanical, photocopying, recording, scanning, or otherwise without written permission from the publisher. It is illegal to copy this book, post it to a website, or distribute it by any other means without permission. Dana Publicover has no responsibility for the persistence or accuracy of URLs for external or third-party Internet Websites referred to in this publication and does not guarantee that any content on such Websites is, or will remain, accurate or appropriate. Designations used by companies to distinguish their products are often claimed as trademarks. All brand names and product names used in this book and on its cover are trade names, service marks, trademarks and registered trademarks of their respective owners. The publishers and the book are not associated with any product or vendor mentioned in this book. None of the companies referenced within the book have endorsed the book.

Cover design by Stephanie Hannus.
Author photo by Chelsea Clayton.

First edition
ISBN: 978-1-79480-208-7

*For anyone who has ever stared at their desk
wondering what they're even doing there,
and who didn't believe they had the power to
change any of it.*

Contents

I:

Understanding Empathy

1

An Introduction to Empathetic Design

How Empathy Solves a Problem

The problem before me was relatively straightforward:
the company was experiencing very low retention in new hires,
specifically in the junior and associate levels, in the age 25–35
demographic. The client and I had gone through a few exercises to
attempt a clear diagnostic and were experiencing a breakthrough. They
just didn't know it yet.

"I think our onboarding might be...boring."

The simple confession, delivered by my client in an almost-
whisper, was met with sympathetic nods around the table. We
were two hours into a four-hour problem discovery workshop—an

intense session during which key stakeholders are brought in to collaboratively identify the root of a challenge, the beginning of a creative problem-solving journey.

I'd been brought in because I had facilitated a brainstorm for a human resources networking group on empathetic hiring processes, and my client had shared the takeaways with her team. They were now trying to incorporate empathy into their own processes.

"I get so many emails and calls with questions asking me who to contact for this, or what's the coverage for that, and people just don't remember what they learned in orientation," the internal recruiter added. "I'm just the recruiter. I don't handle that."

This was it—the moment of discovery. I started to challenge them.

"How do you answer those questions that come in after orientation?" I asked.

"I tell them to check their onboarding packet."

"Why do you think they still have so many questions after orientation?"

"Because they don't pay attention."

"Why don't they pay attention?" I was clearly prodding.

"Because they're looking at their phones."

"Why are they looking at their phones?" I kept pushing.

Exasperated, someone speaks up. "Because the room is a million degrees and they've been staring at a projection all day and we fed them carbs and sugar and talked at them nonstop."

And thus my client had arrived at her conclusion: maybe the onboarding process itself was the problem. I wasn't antagonizing her; the exercise I'd just put her through is the 5 Whys, where instead of accepting a basic explanation or canned answer one asks "Why?" several times until the problem or solution reveals itself.

We reviewed results from the dozens of empathetic interviews my team had conducted prior to the workshop, quotes from which were hung up on the wall as a reminder of the user's (in this case, the new employee's) perspective. People didn't feel a sense of loyalty. They didn't feel welcomed. They didn't feel helped through the process. And they didn't feel informed. Could reworking onboarding solve those problems? Could a new onboarding process be the key to increased retention?

As we worked through the rest of the day's exercises, we developed a problem statement in the form of a "how might we" question: *How might we help new hires to feel loyalty and confidence in their new roles?*

Asking "how" (which solution) "might" (because anything is possible at this point and nothing is out of the question) "we" (because this is collaborative and we're all in it together, equally) is a tenet of empathetic design. Reworking a problem or challenge statement this way keeps focus on solving the right problem, and keeps solutions limitless, broad and open-ended.

To begin to solve this challenge, we needed to empathize even more with new hires.

For this corporate consultation, a team was assembled that involved managers, leaders from different departments, some new hires and longtime employees who matched the demographics of the employees with low retention.

And the first thing I did? Put everyone through the next orientation. Without changing anything.

I invited the team to join a crew of new hires and expanded the invitation to include a few other existing employees, immersing them in the experience we were trying to troubleshoot. Though they were all well-versed in company policies and benefits offerings, my hypothesis was that the information conveyed within orientation itself was not the greatest challenge. For my hypothesis to be true, it would have to mean that the flaw in the experience would transcend their existing knowledge.

After the orientation, all of the participants (including my internal team of problem solvers) were given a quiz with specific questions from the presentations. While some of the information would be common knowledge to a longtime employee, some of the information would not. The results of all tested showed a 70% or less information retention rate. Even those who had been at the company as many as 15 years struggled to recall information they had just learned, even though (according to my friends in human resources) this should all have been common knowledge to any employee.

Quantitative data tells only half the story. To qualify this data, we also interviewed an equal number of existing employees we put through the orientation as well as actual new hires, asking open-ended questions about their experience. This is empathetic research.

Hearing this feedback on everything from room temperature, menu choices, timing, agenda, tone, presentation style and overall program structure resonated with the team. Having been through orientation themselves recently, the team was receptive to receiving this feedback and motivated to leverage it for a creative solution.

The team spent 4 days in a hyper-concentrated development period called a Design Sprint (we'll get to those later) and called back frequently to their recent empathetic experience. I'd also printed quotes from the qualitative interviews and plastered them all over the walls in our Sprint "War Room." During the Sprint, we came up with a new type of onboarding, and on day 5, we tested it with actual new hires.

You read that right. From problem to testable solution in 5 days. And yes, we tested it before we built it. Why?

Traditionally, to solve this problem, the team would have met a few times over the course of a year, perhaps breaking into smaller committees or task forces to tackle different elements of the onboarding process. They would make assumptions about what the new hires thought, or what they needed, or how they might react and make their decisions based on those assumptions.

They would have spent a year designing the ins and outs, the details and infrastructure of a complete overhaul of their onboarding program. Then they would have launched it, with no indication of how it might do or what success would look like, and—due to a lack of empathy—no clear understanding of the actual issue. A very expensive stab in the dark. We could have spent 6 months building new slide decks and recruiting new internal presenters or 9 months finding a new way to deliver the information. We might have even spent 12–18 months building an expensive online app for training[1].

With a smaller investment in time, energy and internal resources—also a greater investment in empathy and validation—the team could have guaranteed the success and outcome of the new onboarding program pre-launch.

---

1 Actual attempted solutions to this problem carried out by other organizations.

This is not rocket science, and it's not magic. Organizational empathy won't have you gathering employees around a campfire and singing *kumbaya*, nor will it have you crying and unpacking feelings about your parents during an annual review. What it will do is change literally every process, program and product of your company—if only you'll let it.

Anything—a product, a service, an experience—can be improved by integrating empathetic research. Research like this has brought us better can openers, nail polish brushes, phones, TVs, MRIs, cars, maps, roads...even government services. In product design, this understanding is fairly commonplace. But I believe there is an opportunity to apply empathy and empathy-based observation to our lives at work, to use the same techniques that have pioneered product design to perfect internal programs like hiring processes, onboarding, wellness programs, innovation departments and even the structure of management. I see your fully blocked calendar as a design flaw, your meeting-that-could-have-been-an-email as a consumer challenge, and your low benefits enrollment as a sales and marketing issue.

As consumers (read: all humans) begin to expect a well-designed user experience as a baseline of all of their interactions—and with company loyalty a non-concern in most employees[2], workplaces must begin to see employees as customers and the working experience as a service if they want to be competitive in the job market. By using product design principles, treating employees like customers and researching their challenges empathetically, companies can design an in-demand workplace that is staffed, productive and desirable. The

---

2 McCusker, Deb & Wolfman, Ilene (1998). Loyalty in the Eyes of Employers & Employees. Workforce.

success of an organization is directly attributed to the performance of its employees[3]. Happy, productive employees who stay long-term serve more than your bottom line—they are your greatest recruiters, marketers, salespeople and public relations agents. This makes empathy your greatest competitive advantage.

3 Murali, Sachin & Poddar, Aayush & Seema, A. (2017). Employee Loyalty, Organizational Performance & Performance Evaluation – A Critical Survey. IOSR Journal of Business and Management (IOSR-JBM). 19. 00-00.

2

Why Empathetic Design Matters

"Empathy is seeing with the eyes of another, listening with the ears of another and feeling with the heart of another." —Alfred Adler

Key Vocabulary:

Empathy (n): the ability to imagine another person's feelings or experience, without explicitly sharing the experience

Sympathy (n): an expression of understanding of another person's feelings that comes from similar or shared experience

An Overview of Empathy

Empathy involves diving deeply into another person's experience so that it becomes your own; being so intimately acquainted with another's feelings that they become yours, or internalizing others' problems so that you understand their full implications. This form of internalizing can lead to a somatic experience or sensation—that is, a physical manifestation that accompanies the experience with which you are empathizing, as though it has happened to you (a jolt in your chest, welling of tears). It is a simulation of the experience, as opposed to the experience (were it to be the actual experience, you would be experiencing sympathy instead). There are people who are naturally more empathetic and who tend to have a greater external awareness of the implications of their own actions, especially as perceived by others, and there are others who are not. I generalize this concept with the following example: there are people who say "I am stuck in traffic" and people who say "I am part of the traffic." There are also people for whom, whether due to a neurological or psychological challenge or something else entirely, empathy is not as accessible.

Empathy comes from the German word *einfühlung*, which means, literally, *feeling into*. There are indications that certain empathetic traits are innate and primitive; for example, the phenomenon of a contagious yawn. We don't yawn on purpose just because we want to. Rather, it's involuntary: the yawn of another person prompts in us an involuntary but equally participatory yawn of our own.

Because the contagion of a yawn is an example of primitive empathy, those with compromised empathic abilities[4] (subjects diagnosed with schizophrenia, those on the autism spectrum or with processing disorders) are far less susceptible to catching a yawn. In

---

4 Provine, Robert R. "Yawning: The Yawn Is Primal, Unstoppable and Contagious, Revealing the Evolutionary and Neural Basis of Empathy and Unconscious Behavior." *American Scientist*, vol. 93, no. 6, 2005, pp. 532–539.

fact, FBI interrogators used to use yawning experiments to determine whether or not their subject was a psychopath.[5] It should be noted that, before you begin testing all of your friends and relatives, this test does not hold up in court.

Empathy is often explained by comparing it to sympathy, yet, even in these explanations, the differences between the two become blurry. Sympathy is best expressed by feeling saddened by someone's sad experience or identifying with their situation (for example, the loss of a pet or a particularly difficult day at work, things that very closely resemble your own experience). Pity and compassion are forms of sympathy. Sympathy in its essence doesn't, therefore, require the participation in another person's experience. Empathy is the elevation of sympathy to a radically different form of experience.

People do not normally need to be taught to feel sympathy. As a mom of twins, I have witnessed first-hand sympathy-based behaviors in my boys at a very early age, usually in the form of sympathetic crying. If one twin is crying for a reason (hunger, dirty diaper, dropped pacifier), there is a moment in which I have observed the other twin register and process this information and cry in solidarity. He doesn't seem to know why his brother is crying but feels compelled to join in; sympathetically, he has cried before for similar reasons. (In fact, for months it was his default. Is there anything worse than a colicky baby? In fact, yes—two colicky babies.)

A great John Steinbeck quote drives this comparison home. He wrote: "It means very little to know that a million Chinese [people]

---

5 Rundle, Brian & R. Vaughn, Vanessa & Stanford, Matthew. (2015). *Contagious yawning and psychopathy.* Personality and Individual Differences, pp 33–37.

are starving, unless you know one Chinese [person] who is starving."[6]
The original quote is more problematic, I'm afraid, but still great (if
indicative of a different time).

Empathy makes another person's problems personal.

Empathy requires that the experience of the other becomes an
experience of one's own.

A quick scroll through our social media feeds bombards us
with photos of weather disasters, of children in peril, the ice caps
literally melting before us, and (perhaps the hardest image of all)
unfortunate dogs. We see these images so frequently that we begin to
scroll past without being moved to action. It is far away. It is someone
else. It is not our fight to fight.

It is not our circus, and definitely not our monkeys.

But what is the first action that a celebrity takes when they
discover their child, their spouse or they themselves have been
diagnosed with a disease? They start a foundation. To care about
something enough to be motivated to act upon it, you must be
personally affected by it. Even Chris Rock has said "If you see me
talking about a disease, I've got it."[7]

It is far more difficult, then, to consciously empathize.
Empathy as this value and practice is not a quality with which we are
born. Babies crying through the night can't shift their perspective to
yours and think, *My poor parents. I can see how exhausted they are.
I'll let them sleep for a few hours.* Making decisions based on empathy
(and thus allowing empathy to drive product development and design)

---

6 Steinbeck, John. *The Grapes of Wrath.* New York: Penguin Classics, 1992.

7 Gross, Terry. "Fresh Air" *Chris Rock On Finding The Line Between Funny And
'Too Far.'* December 2014

requires thinking, and therefore effort. It is not innate.

If this type of empathy, then, is learned—how do we learn it? And before that, how do we even know we are experiencing it? What does empathy *feel* like?

Empathy is that gut-punch realization that you've missed a side of the story. When you become aware of your own limited perspective and have not accounted for an alternative perspective, there's that little zap of awareness. You were operating from your own beliefs and experiences and completely disregarded anything different until this very moment.

There's always a little bit of guilt associated with that realization. It's the first time you realized your parents were actually people—that their existence was not only as an authority over your own life and social calendar. Before you came along, they were probably pretty cool. It's being angry at another person's actions—and then realizing what prompted them to act the way they did. It's awareness of a privilege you were perhaps too privileged to realize you had. That zap of empathy is the sudden feeling of someone else's experience. It's walking a mile in their shoes and feeling their blisters. The simulation of their experience.

While some people are more skilled in empathy than others, no one is a true empath. The majority of people don't walk around feeling all the world's pain and suffering at once and embodying every experience as we go about our day. And no one should be expected to—how awful! But empathy is something we can all use a little more of, and something that can be leveraged for the greater good—even at an organizational level.

Empathy, Institutionalized

Design thinking is built upon empathy. Design thinking, also known as human centered design, is design that prioritizes the experience of the user through empathy of the user's experience in order to solve a problem. It is heavily intertwined with empathy. No doubt you've heard of design thinking before. It's become just another corporate buzzword and is now just shorthand for "a brainstorm with a lot of Post-It Notes." What's been lost in the widespread adoption of design thinking is the empathetic principles upon which it was based—the human centered element of it all, and the problem-solution architecture.

Design thinking in practice is designing a product or service that solves a problem rather than making an assumption of what the market might want. That way, products are validated before hitting the market and launch with assured product-market fit in advance. It's actually quite brilliant.

Designing products and experiences with empathy for the user at the forefront resulted in a paradigm shift from traditional marketing (making people want things) to empathetic development (making things people want). In 1965, Bruce Archer, a mechanical engineer, published *Systematic Method for Designers* which established processes for professional design and also outlined the relationship of design thinking with management. "The time is rapidly approaching when design decision-making and management decision-making techniques will have so much in common that one will become no more than the extension of the other." This was the first use of the term "design thinking" and the beginnings of a framework to design-driven development, which was taken further in architect Bryan Lawson's

1980 *How Designers Think,* widely considered the first instructional design thinking text.

That same year, Apple hired San Francisco design firm IDEO to design the very first computer mouse—one of the first consumer technology by-products of human centered design. Steve Jobs was an early adopter to this empathetic methodology, using it to guide the design of Apple products even in the early years. IDEO, the firm most widely known for implementing design thinking into modern consciousness, is also responsible for the benches you see at the airport just past the TSA checkpoint. They observed travelers at the Oakland airport struggling to put on their shoes after having to remove them during screening. Design thinking really is that simple: solving a small problem with a seemingly obvious solution (put a bench there for people to sit down when they put on their shoes!).

Continuing this work in 1992, Richard Buchanan published an article called "Wicked Problems in Design Thinking." It proposed that design thinking could be used to solve human problems through design. Before design thinking, designers were included only at the end of product development, and typically only with aesthetic decisions that could affect functionality.

As these methods have been embraced, there has been a seat at the table for design much earlier in the process, especially since the 2000s when design thinking became a business buzzword and was seen as a competitive advantage. Companies who idolized Apple were embracing the strategies that helped launch so many successful products, seeing the value of designing with the human user in mind.

Most people acquainted with design thinking now picture a room full of Post-It Notes, a marshmallow prototype or a worksheet.

A departure from routine, but a relatively unproductive practice. That's because design thinking isn't a workshop. It is a mindset and a guiding principle behind everything you do, running constantly in the background and helping to keep projects aligning with goals. You can't just "do" design thinking—you must live it and embody it.

While there was a large organizational shift to include design earlier in the development cycle, empathy and the user's perspective are frequently excluded. Empathy, while once the foundation of the process, has become an inconvenience and the first line item to be chopped. Or, worse—empathetic assumptions are made based on the preferences and experiences of only those who are in the room. Statistically, the top level decision makers are not a diverse group of individuals, meaning this "empathetic" perspective is dangerously limited.

The Empathy Imperative

The need for empathy is undersold as an adult. It is noticeably absent from the workplace and in the way our corporate structures are designed. These decisions are based on the bottom line and the ROI, perhaps even the perspectives of our decision makers. This is precisely why they are not working.

As parents, we make great efforts to equip our children with functional empathy. We guide them through understanding and feeling the experiences of others with phrases like, "How do you think you would feel if Jonah told *you* you couldn't play with his truck?" and "What do you think Anna feels when you tell her she's not invited?" And the tried-and-true go-to of starving children in distant countries: "Can you imagine what it might feel like to go to bed hungry?"

Seriously, I'd be willing to bet there were cave mamas standing over cave toddlers with a plate of uneaten mammoth talking about starving children in other caves. If it is so important for our children to become empathetic, why is it not just as crucial for them to remain empathetic as adults?

While helping a child see situations that are not as desirable as their own can create a sense of empathy (if a bit cautionary), I am not a fan of leveraging another person's misfortune for your own teachable moment. While I do believe in putting your children into experiences that serve to show them that not all lives are like their own—and not all families or homes are like theirs—I disagree with the practice of "volunteering" by having them select their own cast-off toys and outgrown clothing for donation to the less fortunate. I feel like this says to the child that "these people are not as good as we are and so we can give them our garbage." This is not empathy. This creates more of a disparity, a greater divide between "us" and "them." Helping is different.

I've always been fascinated by the Hebrew word *mitzvah*, which simultaneously means *blessing* and *obligation*, and seems to fit so perfectly here. It's a blessing and honor to be able to give time to feed the hungry, and as someone who has that time and money to contribute to the cause, it's also a duty or obligation to help.

In this same way, it is an obligation and a duty to act in empathy. We owe it to our customers, our users, our employees and our fellow humans to listen, to understand their needs and to act upon them.

You know firsthand what an effect an empathetic reaction can have. Have you ever been at a party or networking event where you don't know anyone and are approached by a stranger who makes lively conversation with you? Or been offered a fresh drink right at the exact moment of thirst? Or had someone offer to help you carry a heavy package you are struggling with? It feels good to be seen. It feels like an acknowledgement of our humanity when someone responds to a need we have without being asked.

A well-designed piece of software can have that same effect. Picture it: when you are using a new app and intuitively navigate to something to complete a task, and everything is exactly where you think it should be, doesn't that feel amazing? Don't you feel like a genius? Doesn't that make you feel seen?

If there is actual, tangible data we can gather to help us give others that feeling; if empathetic data to drive our decision-making is available (if we only know where and how to look); and if that information is power to create better, more engaging, more customized and more powerful solutions, certainly it's a *mitzvah* to use it.

3

Empathy in Practice

Surveys are not Empathetic

In the workplace, empathy is an often overlooked (and desperately needed) element in designing solutions. If you want to build successful internal programs, launch successful products or bridge communication gaps, empathy is a *requirement.*

I have worked with clients in many different industries attempting to solve these exact challenges who have projected outcomes, conducted research and invested resources. All the stars were aligned, all elements were in place, all systems were go, and then—nothing. If they were poised for such success, how did they miss the mark?

Within our first meeting, it is often discovered that no one had asked the user: neither about the structure of their experience, past or present, nor about the structure of their need, desire or intent in terms of participation in the structure of a work environment or the consumption of a product.[8] When I point this out, it never fails that an older high-ranking person dredges up the famous Henry Ford quote:

"If I had asked customers what they wanted, they would have said 'a faster horse.'"

Not wanting to make a scene, I don't mention that Henry Ford never actually said that.[9] I do, however, point out the difference between *asking a user* what they want and *asking them about their experience* to spot opportunities and challenges, then to design solutions that better meet their needs. I show them that, by understanding the *problem*, they can come up with much more creative (and much more effective!) solutions. If a solution solves a specific problem for a specific group of people, it has no option but to succeed.

It's like a custom-tailored suit. An idea that fits.

Empathy is not a survey. Nor is it found within one. That's not to say that survey data[10] isn't valuable—it absolutely is! And while new methods of data visualization are helping spot previously overlooked trends to tell more of a complete story beyond just the numbers[11], they're still just numbers.

---

8 In this book, please interpret "user" to mean your employee, customer, student, participant and any other person for whom you may be solving a problem or creating a solution.

9 Vlaskovits, Patrick. *Henry Ford, Innovation, and That "Faster Horse" Quote*. Harvard Business Review. August 29, 2011.

10 We're talking strategically developed surveys capturing scientific data sent to a wide and varied group, not your Google survey.

11 LaValle, Steve; Lesser, Eric; Shockley, Rebecca; Hopkins, Michael S; Kruschwitz, Nina.; Big Data, Analytics and the Path From Insights to Value, *MIT Sloan Management Review*, Cambridge Vol. 52, Iss. 2, (Winter 2011): 21-32.

Empathy research tells us more than that. It tells us things that can't necessarily be quantified. It paints a picture of the experience that allows us to step inside it so that we become intimately acquainted with our user, and create solutions that are truly custom to that user's experience.

A survey doesn't accomplish this. You'll spot some trends and might find some interesting data, but a survey isn't a replacement for empathy. In a survey, you've only provided a handful of quantitative responses, but you've failed to account for outliers, special circumstances and more. Here's a great example, told to me by a colleague of mine who was brought in on a recruitment project. Through their client's survey data they discovered a strange anomaly: approximately ⅓ of their employees had taken more than a month's leave of absence from a job at some point in their life. And just below ¼ had been out of work for between 1–5 years. What the survey failed to capture (and what the in-person interviews did) was that most of these absences were due to maternity leave and mothers who stayed at home with young children.

· To truly *empathize* with the people of your organization, you need to understand them. And to understand them, you need to study them like an ethnographer. Strolling through the factory floor or taking your employees to lunch doesn't fully key you in to their experience (though these are things you should probably do anyway). You need to intimately acquaint yourself with their needs, their challenges and their perceptions.

But I do have empathy for the user—I am the user! Maybe the product you're working on solves a problem you've already had. Maybe before your big promotion you were an entry-level marketing employee, so you should be able to understand their experience. Or perhaps it's even deeper than that: you're creating a new type of accessibility product that you yourself require.

But I already feel empathy for the situation! It's my situation!

Doesn't count. I am sorry to tell you that empathy for yourself is not empathy. You may experience the same problems as your user and have empathy for their situation, but using empathy for yourself to guide your project is not the same as learning about and understanding your users. This self-empathy, though, can be a valuable launching point (*if I am experiencing this, maybe others are experiencing it as well*), and identifying yourself as a power user can help you identify needs early on.

But you won't be buying your own product. Or experiencing your creation as a customer or joining your own program or whatever it is you're working on. By the mere fact of working on it, you're already a contaminated test subject. It's the reason many psychology studies are blind and even double-blind. You are too close to the problem and solution so your mind is already made up. Your opinion doesn't matter.

And then there's the "phone a friend" method of market research. This is where the ambitious and budget conscious (usually students and startup founders) ask their siblings, roommates, moms and fellow cohorts: Would you use this product? Some even take it a step further, crafting an elegant Google form in the middle of the night, sending it out over social media and asking everyone they know to take it. They're crowdsourcing data for their project while sending it only to those they know.

Friends, I don't have to tell you that this is a poor substitute for real research. I also don't need to tell you that empathy is completely missing from the process.

But I asked people what they think! I asked questions and got feedback! That's empathy!

No. Nope. Not even a little bit.

If you build an app that solves your own problem, you manually developed each line of code and each corresponding action. When you use the app, the decisions are intuitive—to you. Empathy for yourself as the user would lead you to believe that everyone would use the app just like you, know exactly where to click and exactly what step to take next.

But your user didn't develop the app. They might not use the same logic you do. An empathy study for usability testing might show you that 90% of your users automatically scroll up to the right first when looking for a button to click. So that's where you put your button. It doesn't matter where you think it should go, your user is giving you the more important information. Unless, like Steve Jobs' custom OS, your product is just for you. In which case, have at it[12].

The good news is that, if your solution has appeal outside of just you, finding a research group whose data will help keep you balanced and open-minded should be easy. And finding empathy for them should also be relatively accessible, since you're mostly there already. You can narrow your focus and even validate your assumptions using empathetic research. And you can ensure a project's success with data gathered through that empathetic research.

---

12 In the early 2000s I met an IT helpdesk employee at Apple who told me that nobody could service Job's Mac because it had a crazy custom operating system. I have been unable to confirm this in my research which is disappointing, because I always thought it was a neat anecdote and have widely (WIDELY) spread it as fact.

How to Become Empathetic

To learn to be empathetic, you need to broaden your perspective. Facebook has long offered "2G Tuesdays"[13] to its employees as a way to empathize with some of the largest new user groups accessing the platform. On 2G Tuesday, employees voluntarily experience a temporary downgrade in mobile access (to 2G) and are able to *empathize* with a group of their users. Silicon Valley–based developers are used to fast 4- and now 5G browsing speeds. But with many new accounts logging in from remote areas with limited web access—most of whom have a 2G connection—it can be difficult to develop apps that work as well in this slowed context. The goal of Facebook's exercise is to create products that work for all their users across all connections, and to see how their products are experienced by users outside of their personal market.

Empathy can be acquired for a specific group (targeting your audience and voluntarily participating in their daily experience) or, more broadly, as a skill. By truly understanding someone else's experience, you can create more meaningful products, services and programs for them that solve their problems—which can lead to things like greater adoption rates, greater sales, increased participation and brand loyalty.

Here are a few ways one can deliberately become more empathetic. These skills will also help you as you move on to conduct your own empathy research (outlined in great detail later in this book).

1. Imagination. Take all of the information you know about a

---

13 Marra, Chris. *Building for Emerging Markets: The Story Behind 2G Tuesdays.* http://code.facebook.com. October 27, 2015.

person's experience as clues to a bigger picture and close your eyes, almost as though you are meditating. Begin to assemble those clues as pieces of a large puzzle and visualize what the complete image looks like. How does their day begin? How do they go about everyday things such as waking up, traveling to work, getting food to feed their family, resting and playing? How does the information you know about them affect their experience in these activities?

2. **Observation.** Go to an unfamiliar place and observe people. See what they do when they think no one is looking. Witness their humanity as they scrape gum from a shoe or use newspaper to dry off a bench. Become absorbed in their experience from afar.

3. **Comparison.** Look for commonalities among your own experiences and those with whom you desire to empathize. Commonalities are everywhere, and even someone whose daily experience seems completely foreign to you has something in common with you. I once was struck with a sudden zap of recognition seeing a woman at a grocery store covered head to toe in a burka lick her thumb and wipe the schmutz from her child's face. I realized—we are both mothers, we are both tired, and we are just trying to get groceries and get home and feed our children. Our experiences are different but overlap much more than I would have thought. Find a shared experience and consider the differences of their version of it.

4. **Interaction**. Seek to meet people who are different from you. Exit your bubble and find those who do not share your experiences, or values, or background, or interests. Engage in

conversations with them. Learn what makes them tick.

5. **Questioning**. Ask questions that reveal insights into a person's experience with genuine interest. Aim to ask more questions than you answer yourself.

6. **Sharing**. Open up authentically and honestly about your own experiences to set the tone for an honest discussion. Make space for others to speak freely, safe from criticism.

7. **Listening**. Perhaps the greatest effort anyone can ever put forth is the act of listening—fully, and without agenda. Internalizing and processing information received and not focusing on formulating a response. Receive, and do no more than that.

8. **Curiosity**. In all of these practices, maintain a genuine curiosity about people. Avoid assumptions and assume you know nothing. Know that those with whom you seek to empathize have all of the answers you need.

II:

Leveraging Empathy

Using Design Thinking to Solve
Problems Empathetically

Key Vocabulary:

Problem Framing: clearly defining and contextualizing a problem and the implications surrounding solving it

Ethnography: the research of people

Ideation: the act of brainstorming or coming up with ideas

Prototype: a crude representation of a finished product that can be tested and iterated without great cost or time investment

Design Thinking 101

This is a crash course to get you up and running (or a quick review for those already in the know). So if your interest is piqued, please read one of the many fantastic and much more heavily researched guides to design thinking written by experts and not by this (evangelizing albeit genuinely passionate) author.

Design thinking workshops and activities always feel a bit like a kindergarten project. That is intentional. When were you at your most creative? When did you believe anything was possible? We become cynical over time, especially in our jobs. We are told no so often that we begin to say it to everything, too. It's easier that way. We lose the fight. We don't ask why, and we don't challenge anything. But (I repeat this constantly, especially in this book), if nothing ever changes, then nothing ever changes.

How can you expect to be truly innovative if you can't change anything?

Design thinking is about asking why, and letting anything be possible in the first creative stages. Ask why. Then ask why again. And again.

This is called the **5 Whys** (remember the onboarding client from before?).

Think of a small child asking why. An answer one layer deep just doesn't satisfy. Why are we in the car? Because we are going to the store. Why are we going to the store? Because we need food. Why do we need food? Because our bodies need nourishment to function. Why do we need to function? Boom. That's quite a powerful question (and kudos to the parent that can answer it). If you ask someone a series of why questions, you tend to dig a lot deeper. It doesn't have to be 5, but that works as a good general guideline.

Often, these questions come after someone says "We have to do it this way," or something similarly locked in traditional thinking. Part of the design thinking process is challenging existing conventions and questioning as much as we can. When we get to an imperative statement, "It must be done this way" or "This is how we do it," there isn't much opportunity for innovation. This is innovation, so the rules are flipped upside down, meaning we have to dig deeper.

"Why does it have to be done this way?" and similar lines of questioning typically lead down a path like this: "Because it has always been done that way." Why has it always been done this way? This question is usually met with silence or a stuttered "I don't actually know…"

Ask why. Keep asking. Question everything.

If you want to solve real challenges in new ways, you need to change your method and your thinking. Challenge all of those answers until a lightbulb goes off and clears the pathway to innovating a solution unhindered by convention. Throw out the rulebook. Get uncomfortable.

Design thinking is about throwing out all the rules, boundaries and conventions. It's seeing the same things in new ways by bending the lines of what's possible.

Here's a quick design thinking exercise: put this book down and cross your arms in front of your chest, like you're exasperated.

Give it a moment.

Okay.

Hopefully you picked the book back up. Now think about the way you've just done that. It's a simple gesture, something you've probably done most of your life, and usually without thinking. You've never realized it, but you cross your arms the exact same way every time.

Now put the book back down again and do it a different way.

Give it a moment.

Okay. Thoughts?

Uncomfortable, isn't it? Probably a bit awkward. That right there is the perfect mindset for innovating. That was your wax on, wax off moment. You are ready.

Designing Experiences

First, understand this: user experience is not limited to apps and digital products. Anything that can be experienced is (earth–shattering reveal) an experience.

To use design thinking in experience design is to form broader questions that leave more room for innovative solutions. Traditional problem solving narrows and narrows our framing of a problem so that the one solution we land on is the only possible option.

By broadening the question, we leave more space for interpretation. For example: if the problem is that people hate waiting to see a doctor, instead of asking, "How can we make people happier while waiting to see a doctor?" we instead would ask "How might we change the experience of visiting a doctor?" Even in this quick example, you can already see the possibility of bigger and better ideas that might have nothing to do with wait time.

It's the Stacy's Pita Chips story, printed right on their bags. The lines at Stacy's sandwich cart were so long, she started bringing out pita chips (a by-product of leftover pita) to those waiting in line. She didn't make the sandwiches any faster, but the people waiting for them had a different experience. Of course, the chips soon overtook the sandwiches and Stacy's Pita Chips was acquired by PepsiCo/Frito Lay for $250 million in 2006. There are infinite ways to solve a problem, but the most effective way is the one that solves it best for the person experiencing it.

The Beginner's Mindset

In the arms-crossing exercise above, how clumsy and new did it feel to have your arms crossed in a new way? Imagine if you had to go about your day crossing your arms the new way, with so little experience. Or using only your non-dominant hand. You'd feel like a beginner, which is the perfect place to start coming up with new ideas.

To achieve a beginner's mindset, the first step is to forget everything you know. You can't solve your problem just by thinking about it more. Seriously, if that were going to work, it would have by now. You're not going to Sherlock Holmes your way out of this by playing the violin and puffing on a pipe until the solution springs to mind.

That's why we use structured exercises designed to help us think differently than we normally do. Part of the reason these exercises tend to spark more ideas than banging your head on your desk is because they start from a place of ignorance. The best way to approach a familiar problem is from a place of ignorance—also known in design thinking as the beginner's mindset.

A beginner's mindset will remove your assumptions, biases and pre-existing knowledge about the problem that blocks you from seeing fresh opportunities. It gets rid of the *but we've always done it this way*s and the *that would never work*s, because without existing knowledge you aren't sure of those two things.

But here's the problem—you already know everything. You live the problem daily and know it inside and out. So how you do look at something so familiar with the fresh eyes of a newbie?

Imagine you didn't know anything. Ask someone else to explain it to you as though you were a child. Ask questions a child would ask. Bonus: explain the problem to an actual child and see if their beginner's mindset drives an interesting line of questioning. You could also try using the 5 Whys.

Or, you could just bring in actual beginners. This may sound like cheat mode but it's very legal and very effective. Multidisciplinary teams have many benefits, the most obvious being an outsider's perspective. By bringing together people who are not close to the problem, you broaden the opportunity for solutions. This is the role I most frequently play with my clients. It's called thought partnership; it brings in the outsider's perspective and provides a sounding board. Sometimes just talking it through with someone helps you understand it from a different angle. It's the benefit of an entire person's experience and knowledge focused on something you understand deeply.

Something I use to help people who seem to be biased to a solution already in their minds is to set limitations on the types of solutions during a brainstorm. With rules or parameters to guide your thinking, you block off familiar and easy solutions, removing the internal limitations you subconsciously already live by. Limitations can help you think of your problem from a different perspective or change the rules to change the outcome. This has worked so well for people I've worked with that I've started printing these limiters on a deck of cards and handing them out when our work together is done to help them maintain momentum. An example of a limitation (a card in the deck) would be "How would you solve this problem without using technology?" or "How would you solve this problem if it did not have to be profitable?" In design thinking, there are no bad ideas because so frequently a silly or totally impractical idea has sparked inspiration for a completely innovative and feasible concept.

The Design Thinking Process

Design thinking has five phases. They are:

1. **Empathize.** This is the first and most important step, and your research phase, during which you make sure that you're solving the right problem in the first place, solving it for the right people, and solving it well. This is done best through ethnographic research and empathetic interviewing. Through gaining understanding of the root nature of the problem, you'll be much better suited to generate solutions for it. You'll also have first-hand accounts to guide the creation.

2. **Define.** Now that you have a clearer understanding of the source of the problem, you can define your problem more clearly and begin to define the needs for your solution. This will be expressed in a "how might we" question, which will simultaneously narrow the focus and broaden the possibility for solutions.

3. **Ideate.** This includes brainstorming as many ideas as possible, with nothing excluded for reasons of being impossible, impractical or ridiculous.

4. **Prototype.** We aren't building launchable rockets here. We're building low-resolution prototypes that are testable. Instead of building a website, we're creating digital images (or even paper mockups) of what the website might look like and how a user might flow through it. Instead of a robot that serves poolside drinks, it's Tim from R&D wearing a cardboard robot costume. If too many resources are invested in a prototype that won't solve a problem, it's harder to go back to the drawing board. We need to fail fast, and the fastest way to

fail is a low-resolution test.

 5. **Test.** Another opportunity for empathy. Have real users test your fake product. Take as many notes as possible.

 6. **Iterate.** Absorb feedback from the test. Process this information and use it to guide your next prototype(s). Keep going through the process again and again, failing faster and faster until you stop failing.

5

How Empathy Can Help You Fail
Better (and Faster!)

Key Vocabulary:

> *Validation: confirmation in the validity of an idea*
>
> *Failure: validation that something will not work*
>
> *Rapid or early validation: like a crystal ball, the upfront knowledge that a solution solves a particular problem or meets a market need, usually achieved through user testing or prototyping before the end product has been built*
>
> *Low resolution: like a pixelated image, a lesser-quality version than the real thing (for example: paper mockups of app screens, a row of chairs to represent a school bus, or a foamcore scale replica of the interior of a store)*
>
> *Divergent thinking: an unrestricted brainstorming process in which quantity of ideas is prioritized and there are no limits on the type of idea generated in order to explore many possibilities*

Convergent thinking: a brainstorming process where the focus is to come up with a streamlined, thorough and executable idea

How to Fail Faster

Sometimes, for new clients, I'm brought in as a last resort, a life raft to salvage a failing project ready to be written off. It's already been deemed a failure; the stakeholders have abandoned it to avoid having a failure attached to their names, resources have been cut off and the bleeding project has been passed into new (lower-ranking) hands. The exciting prospect of these new hands is that they often belong to someone who is familiar with my work in solving problems quickly and with lean resources, the hands of someone who isn't afraid to try a little outside-the-box thinking. With low stakes, and even lower resources, we have space to experiment.

This trial by fire is an opportunity to validate my work and hopefully earn a spot on a higher-stakes project down the line—it also serves as an excellent case study for a fast failure, a low-cost prototype and using new techniques. If we can do this with about $60 in materials and no support, think of what we can do with more!

There is a way to know if a project would be successful before it's even started. It's fast, it's low stakes and it's supported by data. It's validation.

In the onboarding example earlier in this book, I posited that following traditional methods would have rebuilt the model of orientation over the course of a year without actually knowing how it would work. Suppose they had gone about it that way, and six months later saw no change in their employee retention rates. Project failure.

Time wasted. What now?

Often, this is when I enter the scene. Because of the work I do, new clients are often skeptical to include my methods into a budget for a project already off to a great start. However, when I can resurrect a dying project using these methods, I usually create lifelong fans of fast failure and die-hard devotees who can't launch a project without it.

In the consultation for the failing project, the client will explain broadly how this doomed project was poised for success. They never fail to mention how much money has already been invested, and how many hours of meetings have already been put in—as though a project's guarantee of success is wrapped up in either of those variables. I can assure you, *it is not.* I have seen companies spend very little time and very little money and launch an insanely popular product (Warby Parker, for example). Conversely, I have seen limitless funds and years of devotion launch a disappointing product (anyone still using—or ever used—Google Plus?).

Sunken Cost Fallacy: The Opposite of Failing Fast

We need to stop associating a project or an idea's value solely with how much we have invested into it, in the sense that the investment placed into a product or otherwise should always be proportionate to an evaluation of its true potential, as guided by empathetic-based design thinking.

Given the state of modern corporate development, this type of thinking requires a paradigm shift that is extremely difficult to communicate to professionals raised in that mindset. There are those who come from a place of abundance and access that know that, if you throw enough money at a problem, it *will* get solved. But most companies are no longer (or never have been) in a position to hemorrhage resources just to achieve project closure. They embrace an "it doesn't have to be perfect, it just has to be done" mentality that can't possibly result in a win.

"We've spent so much money on this. Why doesn't it work?"

The money and time investment is also detrimental to the possibility of a pivot—especially a dramatic one—since people can see a pivot as backtracking. Changing the method (or the goal) is thus seen as floundering, or wasting work that's already been done.

There is a difference between floundering and pivoting. Larger companies still seem to operate under a *don't change horses mid-stream* mindset. Traditionally, if a company were to jump from solution to solution without ever fully launching a completed product, it would appear as though they did not know what they were doing. But now pivots are expected—and in many cases necessary. And the ability to re-pivot is essential.

Think of what would have happened if just two years after manufacturing the first Model Ts, Ford had pivoted to pharmaceutical delivery. No one would have taken them seriously. But now Apple is entering the healthcare space and Google is building cars. In a crazy series of pivots and backtracks, you can now buy books from Amazon in a physical retail location—remember when Amazon was *just* an online bookstore putting all of the brick-and-mortar bookstores out of business?

Not all pivots are successful. Remember when Michael Jordan played baseball? But pivoting is an opportunity to bail out—ideally early enough to recover, or pre-emptively enough to help—and often the only way a company can maintain relevance and a competitive edge.

Commitment to a bad project means even more time and resources must be dumped into reviving it, even when it's already been identified as a probable failure. Those involved feel that to recoup their losses (or have something to show for their investment), the show must go on.

Instead, knowing when to cut your losses and move on— and knowing how to find that next step or identify the pivot—is of incredible value. Learning how to develop and launch new products in a more hypothetical or beta-like space in order to test and validate assumptions—*without* the enormous resource investment—means being able to take bolder risks with a bigger safety net.

This is known as *failing fast,* or rapid validation.

How More Failures Will Prevent Major Failures

We need to embrace the F word. Frequent failures are small. Failing in a rapid and resource-light environment means you successfully avoided a grand failure and invested very little before validation. You haven't lost much time *or* money. You now know it won't work—and you probably know why.

If things can be developed to a point where they can be tested quickly, with a lean team and limited resources, they can be proven or disproven quickly. A pivot at this point—or iteration, or going back to the drawing board—isn't cutting your losses. It's learning from mistakes, creating new assumptions and arming your team with the knowledge they need to dust off and try again. It is the iterate step in design thinking. It's part of the process, not a deviation from the plan.

Most projects will not end up anything close to the first

iteration. In the dozens of Design Sprints I have facilitated, the solution voted on during the Sprint to be worked on by the team has never been what we launch. But there is a kernel of inspiration in that solution; it's a ghost of the final product. A distant cousin many generations back. The key is to make sure everyone on the team understands this and does not become married to the solution that day. It will change—many, many times—and the change is going to happen quickly—very, very quickly—so that Sprint newcomers may feel frustrated or that their heads are spinning trying to keep up.

In a *fail fast* environment, you might not have completed projects to showcase as a trophy or even tangible proof of your hard work. Instead, success can be measured in time saved, assumptions re-evaluated, knowledge or experience gained, or a new idea (or a volume of ideas).

It takes my clients an adjustment period to be able to use the word *failure*. In a corporate environment, we are used to calling problems "opportunities" and avoid any negative terms, especially a concept with time and money devoted to it. But, to innovate, we must embrace and become accustomed to failure.

After all, it takes many failed attempts to create a simply brilliant idea. It took Dyson 15 years and 5,127 prototypes to launch the first Dyson Cyclone Vacuum (see, your failed project doesn't seem like such a huge waste of resources now, does it?). Thomas Edison claimed to have found "10,000 ways that won't work" as a lightbulb.

Fast failure and empathy are linked more closely than you think.

Rapid Validation with Empathy

Think back to my clients, bringing me in to help revive (or extinguish) that failed project. I conduct a rather informal post-mortem process (that is, an autopsy of how this project died—morbid, I know). I ask several questions to dig deeper into what was considered, what research was done, and what assumptions were made.

And that's where it happens. Frequently enough not to be a coincidence.

I ask about the user. They tell me about their market research or their surveys, sometimes even a focus group. They polled their peers. They considered their demographics. But not one of those tools includes true empathy for the user.

Let me clarify: I'm not trying to discount years of refining algorithms, statistical analysis, and research substantiated by buying habits and consumer information. In fact, I believe those are very helpful tools. They do not tell the complete story, however. They are only one piece of the puzzle, and relying on them as your singular resource for developing a new product is like drawing a map of what the rest of the United States probably looks like when all you've seen is the East Coast. You need the full picture. You need all the information.

An on-demand economy and a saturated marketplace have spawned a new breed of consumer that expects solutions to be customized specifically to their needs—and not just at the luxury level. To stand out among competitors, it's necessary to put the user first when developing products and services. Market research and demographics alone will not hold the information you need to create a competitive product. You need to go deeper.

Empathy is the key to that level of understanding. Researching, observing and becoming intimately acquainted with your user will guide your solution and ensure it meets their needs.

So how will empathy help you fail faster?

The quickest way to fail is to invalidate an assumption. Acting on these assumptions without testing or validation early on in the process—and without appropriate empathetic research—means letting a potentially inappropriate or misaligned solution travel further down the pipeline. It's doomed from the start, and it's going to drag your resources along with it.

The absence of user empathy is not the only reason a project can fail. However, many failures could be prevented (or pivoted) by adding empathy early in the process, and validating assumptions by testing with your users.

Problem Framing: Solving the Right Problem

"A problem well stated is a problem half-solved." —*Charles Kettering*

I was working with a team who had created a product for IT professionals. Their product was testing extremely well with target users, but sales were a bit flat. Before bringing me onboard, the CEO—nervous about running out of runway—sent a survey to two groups of people: those who had purchased the product in the last 6 months and those who had requested more information on the website without a purchase.

The survey he'd assembled asked questions like "how much do you normally spend on software licenses annually?" and "what would you pay for this product?" Because he had many leads and a low close rate, he assumed his cost was too high and people dropped out of the funnel once they had that information. Thus, all of his survey questions were related to cost.

I was brought in to run a brainstorm session where the problem statement given to me by the CEO was:

How might we educate the customer on the value of the product so that they understand everything they get for the purchase price? (Actually, "How can we convince them it's worth it without changing our cost?")

Leading up to the brainstorm session, I reviewed the survey results with his team and gathered information about the sales process. The survey data seemed to be missing a few key pieces of information, so I proposed we dig deeper with a few survey respondents. We conducted a few brief interviews about the sales process itself, asking open-ended questions in an effort to understand—and empathize— with their experience.

In the first interview, we learned something interesting. The user, the one who would serve as admin and point of contact on the product, who would own the product internally, did not have purchasing authority. And because of the hierarchical structure at this particular company, the purchaser did not understand the user's need for the product.

Six sessions later, we had a trend. Our user was not our buyer, and our buyer did not understand the point of our product. The problem was not the cost.

If we had based our next steps on the survey results and the assumed problem, we would have invested time and money into a solution for that problem, and without empathetic validation we would have launched that solution unsuccessfully. We would have solved the wrong problem.

Validation is the premonition that tells you how things will probably go. It's as close as you can get to a crystal ball, and it's something left out of the process so frequently it doesn't make sense. Once we had an idea of the real sales issue, our brainstorm session was devoted to prototyping a few solutions. Some of us would test a new set of sales materials, and some of us would test a completely different outreach process. Both of these were tested with users who had requested more information on the website, so they had already entered the sales funnel. It was a small-scale test since these were just prototypes and not fully developed solutions. But the test showed us which parts were working, which meant when we built the final solution, we already knew what would happen. We saved time (from interview to prototype to test to actual launch was within a month) and we had empathetically led validation that our users' problems would be solved.

To properly frame a problem, it's essential to dive deep into exploring all possible angles, gathering as much information as possible, and uncovering the consequences of both solving it and leaving it unsolved. The context of your problem will help you make sure it's the right problem to solve, that it's not a symptom or by-product of a greater issue. You'll know the problem is framed when it can't be simplified any further—when the 5 Whys don't give you any new information and when you can't find any other underlying reasons to explain the problem.

People—especially the type of passionate people you hope to be working with—will care about the problem and their involvement with it. They may take things personally, especially if they feel they are to blame for any part of the problem. It's important to keep the reason for solving the problem, and the person for whom you are solving it, top of mind. Bringing emotions into solving a problem is something that should be embraced, not discouraged. This is a huge shift in thinking from traditional work meetings, but passion and friction are key to problem solving.

The Importance of Friction

A heated, passionate debate where feelings begin to get involved is friction. A disagreement where people find themselves fighting for their ideas or beliefs is friction. At just a whiff of this friction, most meetings are stopped by the leader and everyone is told to calm down. But stopping this friction is like stopping two sticks rubbing together—the spark is about to happen, but you're preventing it.

That passion means people care about the problem they're solving—and caring more can be a direct result of (or impetus for) empathy for the user. Passion will drive this project forward. Do not stop passion. Do not give passion a cold shower. Embrace it, encourage it, and let it burn, baby!

Friction is multiple viewpoints bumping against each other to accomplish a compromise. If everyone agrees, something is missing. There is a Hebrew parable that says if a jury of rabbis all agree, then they are missing something important. Without discourse and disagreement, the ideas go unchallenged and are not explored from every angle. To completely understand a subject is to argue about it, so friction is a necessity.

Friction is an essential part of the creative ideation process and can be intentionally introduced by creating interdisciplinary teams—which happens to be another cornerstone of design thinking. No one job function, role or title owns creativity (even you, Creative Department. Sit down). In fact, bringing in those that have no stake in the problem, no experience in the field, and completely different perspectives both inspires more friction and yields more varied solutions (remember your beginner's mindset? Doesn't this all fit together so nicely?).

Think about it: if you wanted to create a new type of motorcycle and brought in a motorcycle builder, designer and rider, you would probably get a creative version of an existing product. But what if you brought in a data scientist, an architect, a cyclist, a motorcycle owner and an appliance manufacturer? What kind of product might you end up with?

Friction naturally occurs when multiple people are gathered, but if you find your meeting feeling a little less than passionate, there are things you can do to spice it up.

1. **Ask direct questions meant to challenge assumptions.** If someone makes a statement that is unsubstantiated, ask them why they think that (maybe a good opportunity for the 5 Whys?) or what is causing it. Ask what they have done to try to solve it or clarify it.

2. **Ask "What if the opposite were true?"** Asking people to think hypothetically can help shift conversation in a new direction and also lead to disagreement—which you very much want! Challenging an existing notion with a hypothetical opposite is a way to break these patterns of

thinking.

3. **Create tension by encouraging honesty.** We tend to avoid this type of conflict in the workplace, but, by creating a safe space that allows for free expression of personal opinion, you can nurture friction. Ask stakeholders to help you with this part by setting the tone for authenticity. Ask leaders to share honest feedback and thoughts with the group. You can also ask questions that illicit this type of response during breaks or pre-meeting, and then bring them up with the group later. "During the break, I was speaking to a few of you and it seems like a lot of you feel that the current process is unproductive. How many of you feel that way?" Feeling as though their opinions may be mainstream, people may speak up. Ask for individuals to share thoughts with the group that were shared with you.

Friction in Divergent & Convergent Thinking

There are two ways to come up with ideas: divergent thinking and convergent thinking. Both of these are phases in the human centered design process and occur twice in the cycle. And both of them are areas where friction churns. You need both of them—you must go wide before you can go narrow.

Divergent thinking is always first and occurs when the question is broadened to allow for many different types of ideas. "How might we change the experience of going to the doctor?" would kick off divergent thinking. Ideas fly in all directions and cover many areas; some realistic, some ridiculous.

Once these ideas are gathered, it's time to begin sorting them through discussion and debate. People are invested in their ideas. They feel strongly about their solutions to the problem, including what should not be a solution. Friction drives this debate. As the ideas begin to converge into potential solutions, your team is using convergent thinking. Convergent thinking begins to apply logic and analysis to perception and preconception.

At this point it makes sense to begin to narrow the question to help the convergence, looking for trends among the ideas and guiding them into a group of solutions.

Because the team you've gathered has all key stakeholders in the room (because you've taken all of my advice and planned this thing expertly, haven't you!), it will begin to act as one operating brain that is both creating and debating itself. Then it will be able to approve and enact solutions. If facilitated properly and with balance, the friction will never overpower the room to create a negative atmosphere, and your team will be able to function creatively and critically simultaneously.

Here's where bringing in an external facilitator (oh hi!) can be an incredible asset. They are removed enough from your problem that the solution isn't personal. They can keep conversation productive and make sure all voices are heard equally, that no one hogs the floor. They have no preconceived notions about what your solution should be, so they cannot advocate for their own agenda in a way that steers the conversation toward one concept. They are an ally for process, a ruthless timekeeper (some of us, at least) and have an expert sense of when it's time for a snack break (again, just one of my many life skills).

The divergent-convergent process remains simple, direct

and open for creation. It is repetitive and easily reproduced. There is comfort in the procedure because there is so much discomfort elsewhere. The agenda never changes, but the ideas and solutions do wildly.

Friction and discomfort are what make these processes work. Even just allowing the friction to occur and helping steer it back toward convergent thinking in the end is new territory for most people. Embrace discomfort, just as you're embracing all the other new ways to approach problem solving in this book. Because, I'll say it again, if nothing ever changes, then nothing ever changes.

The Design Sprint

These methods come together inside of a Design Sprint, which is a condensed period of ideation and development where a team solves a real problem by creating a real solution that is then validated with real users. Pioneered by Google Ventures and created by Jake Knapp (you can learn this methodology directly from Knapp in his book *Sprint!* in far more depth than I intend to give you here), the Design Sprint has been embraced by companies that include Virgin, Uber, Slack, Verizon, Wells Fargo, Tesla and even the US Government. A Design Sprint can be adapted for almost any industry and almost any challenge.

The Design Sprint is traditionally 5 days, though many practitioners including myself have shifted to a 4-day model. The day is very structured with workshops and guided discussion. Feedback loops are broken. Phones are left outside the room (I'm serious!). The guest list is limited, and very exclusive.

Typically, the Sprint includes designers, marketers and

salespeople, but it can include engineers, IT, accountants or literally anyone else. The first two days are a workshop, followed by a prototyping day and a testing day. The team agrees on a solution by the end of day two, and a low-resolution (fast failure!) prototype is built and tested with real users. Empathetic research leads the beginning and end of the week. There is friction, convergence, divergence, liminal space and mountains of Post-It Notes. The Design Sprint is empathy in action.

In a corporate, internal Design Sprint, 5 straight days of collaboration is a scheduling nightmare. I've adapted the process for clients so they are present for the first day or two (the workshop part) while my team builds the prototype, runs the test and reports back. I do not recommend breaking the 5 days up into 1 weekly phone call for multiple weeks (buy me a drink and I'll share an anecdote on this one…). While this can work remotely (and many teams do remote-only Sprints), I find there's nothing to replace that in-the-room energy. I've also adapted this process into smaller half-day workshops, and while there's no substitute for a week of innovating, the methods from a Design Sprint can be used as parts of a whole to show progress to a team when all hope seems lost.

The tragic flaw of the Design Sprint is what happens after the week. Such fantastic momentum deserves a handover of sorts, and many colleagues of mine have shared takeaways on how this process should go. We all seem to agree on one thing: the Design Sprint is not an end-all solution but an excellent start. In fact, the Design Sprint has so much flexibility and is such a phenomenon that there is a group of practitioners I'm honored to be included among that meet annually to discuss updates in the process, new learnings and methodologies at

Google. Each year I leave SprintCon (oh yes, it's that serious) with a renewed love for design thinking, the Design Sprint and the power of people to design change—along with a host of new techniques to try out on my clients back home.

The Design Sprint can be done by anyone brave enough to read the book and lead the charge, or it can be facilitated by a professional (again, hi!). It's not a magical cure-all tonic, but it's the perfect combination of everything in your empathy toolbox to help you solve and validate solutions to your challenge.

III:

Scaling Empathy

*"Organizations don't change.
The people within them do."*

6

Employees as Users

"Customers will never love a company until employees love it first."
—SIMON SINEK

Key Vocabulary:

Intrapreneurship: a department or arm of an organization operating as a startup; internal to the greater organization

Innovation Lab: a testing ground for new ideas, explored internally at a company but often outside of traditional company practices

Who owns change?

Unless you're in a leadership role, you probably don't feel that you're able to make much of a difference in your company's culture. Or in anything at all. But the people at the top aren't able to take as many risks as the people in the middle. They're also too far removed from the general employee experience to be aware of most of it. It's those with boots on the ground who are able to make the most powerful and long-lasting changes. I call these people change makers, and they're the ones poised to carry out the great coming workforce revolution.

Maybe you're not ready to take on organizational change. Or maybe you don't care about changing the greater corporate culture but you'd like to take a lunch now and then and not have to call in to meetings on your vacation. Even those not in a position of power have the ability to make these transformations.

Workplaces know they have a recruiting issue. The truth is that they need you more than you need them. The cost of employee turnover can't be ignored. Studies show it can cost 16% of the annual salary of an employee to lose them (losses calculated include time training them, lost productivity due to decrease in job satisfaction prior to vacating the given job, seeking and interviewing, then training an employee replacement). The costs are higher for higher ranking employees. Could an empathetically designed workplace and culture be the key to higher retention? (Spoiler alert: definitely.)

Without employees, you have no customers.

Without satisfied employees, you may have deeply unsatisfied customers.

Post-recession, teams run with skeleton crews. After watching companies launched in dorm rooms by nerds in sweatshirts take over the world, large companies trying to survive the recession made cutbacks under the guise of operating lean (like a startup!). Just like at a startup, employees wear many hats, their responsibilities cover many areas, they work inhumane hours with the expectation of being always-on, and teams that would have originally boasted 20 members are closer to 5–6. The fat has been trimmed.

This doubling- and even tripling-down on roles while adding countless hours to the work week means that employees are overburdened with details, overworked and expected to keep coming up with fresh ideas.

In fact, because they are balancing so many different responsibilities, employees play a greater role in the development of new solutions. Every team is an R&D team. Employees are expected to contribute creatively and participate in the innovation process, with companies like Black & Decker, L'Oreal, and Cisco launching *intrapreneurship* programs—internal processes for employee-submitted ideas—and innovation labs. Proctor and Gamble's P&G labs has been the most successful of these initiatives. In these internal programs, employee ideas are handled like startup pitches with the company acting as investor and launching micro-companies under their corporate umbrella, often outside of their own industry. The company creates an atmosphere primed for the next Post-it Notes[14] while employees find yet another expectation added to their mammoth list of responsibilities.

Many companies take this "walk like a startup" thing a bit further, giving employees unlimited free snacks, fun couches, ping-pong tables, jeans on Friday and brightly colored walls sure to help inspire creativity. By making your company look like Pixar on the inside, it seems only natural that the brilliant ideas would start flowing.

---

14 We all know the story of Post-It Notes' accidental creation by a low-ranking 3M employee.

But most companies stop there.

Even internally, when you build something for someone else, the empathy component is *crucial*. An internal product is still a product. The mistake many companies make is to not treat their employees like customers or users. They make sweeping assumptions about what employees want based on their own wants, or what they think they know about the types of people in their employ. Decision makers within a large company have a very linear set of expectations when it comes to employee reward: we did XX for them, therefore they will do XX for us.

Gary Vaynerchuk, the over-the-top evangelist of digital marketing, has a well-proven theory about this give and take which he outlines in his book *Jab, Jab, Jab, Right Hook!* The Cliff's Notes version: when you give something freely and generously, you create an emotional contract with that person, a sense of obligation on their end.

By example: if you give a free e-book (jab), a series of videos explaining how things work (jab), a welcoming experience and high-end snacks in your showroom (jab), you've established a very one-sided relationship of giving that makes most humans feel uncomfortable. By this overwhelming generosity, when you finally deliver your ask (right hook!), the ask creates a feeling of obligation and owing something in return, often resulting in a customer making a purchase.

We've seen this work incredibly well in digital marketing. Companies and brands that invest energy into informative and educational content—content that feels mostly objective and serves to educate the user about the product or industry in general—see efforts translate directly into sales. Educating your potential user on how products like yours work establishes you as an expert, fills a need the user has, and positions you as the best resource for the product.

Looking back at the corporate example, it seems like there's a significant ask with little reward. The ask (take on more responsibilities, work longer hours, answer emails at night *and* come up with a billion dollar idea) seems a little out of touch with the give (here are some snacks, keep your job [maybe], and we'll print your name in the company newsletter for your idea). While there are companies that certainly don't fit within this exaggerated example, there are plenty of companies whose intrapreneurship programs seem to fall a bit short.

When developing an internal program, whether for wellness, intrapreneurship, career advancement, recruiting or charitable giving, many companies forget to treat the employee as a customer. But if the program is for them, and the goal is to make it work for them, they become your user. And we've already established that empathy is required to create a solution that works for a specific user group.

So how do you garner empathy for employees?

It starts very simply. You see these people every day. You spend more time with them than with your own family. But do you really know them?

Think of the last time you truly listened to them. Not office-listened, but listen-listened. Have you asked them questions that help you better understand their experience? How is their experience in the office different from yours? Do you have certain privileges that they do not have? Do they have certain struggles or fears that you do not? What would it be like to have those?

If you are a manager, think about managers you've had. Think about being at your employees' level. Wrap yourself in that experience and relive it.

Managers and high-ranking professionals seem to fall victim to role-based amnesia shortly after promotion. The shift in power dynamic disrupts their ability to relate to those working under them. It makes sense—often, they are put in place to manage people they once worked side-by-side with. The relationship has to change and they need to assert clear authority.

If this describes you, let it go. Remember what it felt like when your boss came up behind you at your desk—that panicked moment where you quickly inventoried what tabs you had open, and the fear that you didn't look busy enough. And remember what you felt like when your boss came by at 4:55 on a Friday and dumped a stack of work onto you—*seriously?!* Think about how your first few years on the job were spent vying for some sort of recognition, some validation that you were important, essential, valuable (outing myself as a Millenial here, and letting you know that your employees under age 40 all probably feel like this).

Now, while feeling all of these things, and beginning to understand the experiences of those around you, how motivated are you to spend your "free" time participating in a corporate program? Feeling stretched thin and stressed, what is your response to a request for further work beyond your usual duties—especially when that work is expected to be fresh and creative?

I ask: What kind of internal program do you want to build? How will it serve your employees? How will it fill their needs or solve their problems? If the solution first and foremost serves the company—quite transparently—it will always feel like a right hook.

Where is your jab? What's in it for them?

The most successful corporate wellness initiatives reward participants where it matters most: the wallet. The company benefits by having fewer at-risk employees and the employee benefits with lower premiums. Employees are happy to quit smoking, lower their cholesterol or lose weight if it means they'll be paid to do so. They'll also reap the rewards of a healthier lifestyle.

Not all internal programs have an obvious physical benefit or can use a monetary incentive to increase participation. There also might be legal reasons where money is not an option.

So what is as good as money to your employees? It may be different at every location. It may even be different from department to department.

The only way to find out what your employees would want is to ask them. Conduct an empathy study (again, a survey will not suffice) and try to understand their needs, wants, interests and values. Just ask them.

Create a program around their unique values, not just what competitors are doing or what market research tells you your employees want. Take the amazing opportunity you have to interview your own user (How great is that? They're right there!) and don't feel the need to conceal your reasons for the empathy study.

IDEO's Managing Director Bryan Walker developed a course on building internal momentum. He wrote that the key is to bring people into the fold early and often. He called them evangelists.

"People support what they create," he said.

People are much more willing to support an initiative in which they have a stake. By bringing them into the process and putting the emphasis on their contribution, you make these persons part of the development in a real way. You show that you value their input and plan to use what they say to guide the creation of this program. Employee buy-in is crucial to the success of any internal initiative.

Evangelists are also an excellent way to garner internal program support, and they can serve as double-agents as you seek to empathize with and communicate to people in other departments. Consider adding representatives from each area or department as you embark on your empathy study: perhaps shift leaders, project managers, team coordinators and other mid-level employees. You should avoid upper management but also select people with slightly more experience than an entry-level. Someone who is knowledgeable about the functions of their team but not a decision maker.

Educate these evangelists on your goals and your plan to achieve them. Then enlist their help in rallying their teams around the new program. They will have the greatest insight into the best ways to communicate with employees—and may be willing to share profound and candid feedback as you establish a trusting relationship.

Part of accessing this valuable, honest feedback is creating a forum in which it can be freely shared. Again, a survey (or its even lesser cousin, the suggestion box) is insufficient in gathering true data. And while many companies have "town hall" meetings, employees rarely feel confident or comfortable sharing their true feelings—or asking their real questions. The stakes are much too high. People won't risk their jobs or reputations for honesty, but without it, you'll never have the answers you need for healthy structuring and re-structuring.

Use your evangelists to set a precedent for safely shared feedback that gets results. Meet with them frequently and share with them honestly. Make them feel valued and trusted. Confide in them and help them to feel valued as part of the process, not just as recipients of content or questions but as active participants in the shaping of the construction of the programming before them. The relationship will become reciprocal and they will begin to share with you. Use this information to create easy wins early on and bring your evangelists into the spotlight: solve one of their problems or use one of their suggestions. Feature them. Tell everyone. Soon, more suggestions will follow.

A caveat here is to make sure you are not setting up a system of tattletales. Your evangelists should not be coming to you to report employee misdeeds, nor create a system where that is expected. Feedback is not snitching. It should not be rewarded.

The trust in this relationship is incredibly important. You bring them into the fold and you are being very transparent with them—do not betray their trust when they are straightforward with you. Word will spread quickly and you will lose any honest feedback going forward.

By seeing employees as a customer to be marketed to, sold to and onboarded to your product (the company, the department, the program), you can now create a workplace empathetically designed with their needs in mind.

The Empathetic Workplace

I have a semi-regular dinner with friends who work in design and design-adjacent roles. After the general catching up with personal lives, the discussion always turns towards work. We're all very busy, after all, because we are hardworking women who love what we do. But every once in a while I hear something like this that breaks my heart:

"They cut department budgets so we don't get catered lunches anymore. Now I sit through a 2-hour lunch meeting with no food."

I thought she was exaggerating, but she wasn't. Her company had suspended lunch spending but continued to schedule meetings through lunch hour. She told me no one in her department takes lunch in order to gain an extra hour in the work day, that no one leaves at 5pm, and that most everyone logs back on after dinner at home.

I asked her how many hours most people work, in general, and her guess was above 60 a week. Not just the senior level but associates and juniors as well.

"On top of that, I'm expected to spend 20% of my time on future planning, but that always gets pushed because something's always on fire."

Here is something I wish I had known when I was in the corporate grind: There is no glory in Karoshi (過労死), translated literally from the japanese as *overwork death*. If it regularly takes more than 40 hours a week to do your job (and you are not an executive), it is a job for more than one person. You are filling two roles and should be paid double, given personnel support or have your responsibilities more reasonably divided.

This is something you can absolutely control and absolutely change, without losing your job. Employees do not see their own position of power. We're still burned from job searches back in 2009, or of horror stories of friends who were out of work for years. We know we can't afford to buy our own health insurance (in the US), so we give more of our lives and our wellbeing over to a company we know would cut us loose at the first opportunity. But would they, really? Or do they need us too badly?

Do you know anyone who has set boundaries for themselves at work? Someone who has said they don't respond to emails received after 5pm? For most roles, these boundaries are well within your right as an employee and could be the determining factor between you having a life outside of work, and not. Does it say anywhere in your employee handbook that vacation time is still considered working hours? Or that lunch is optional?

It is not too late to start creating these boundaries, whether you've worked somewhere 14 days, 14 months or 14 years. You are a human being, not a machine. You are capable of great work and contributions to your company, but you cannot do that if you are exhausted, hungry or burnt out. Know what you need to bring your best, and know what you are unwilling to compromise on. Recognize that your conditions may be inhumane, and take action to remedy them today.

As a company, recognize when this is happening to your employees. Signs of burnout are easy to spot.

Make room for the 20%

In ideal conditions, many senior roles are expected to spend approximately 20% of their time coming up with new ideas, strategizing and planning. But, as experienced by my dear friend on the toxic team, when everything is an emergency (incidentally, symptomatic of a lack of planning and strategy…) the 20% strategy time is the first thing to go. As though this is a luxury or fluff item and not an absolute necessity!

Because strategy and planning can be difficult to define (and because it often doesn't look as busy as other work), we can let it slip through the cracks in favor of tangible, completable tasks. Make it tangible by blocking off time on your calendar for it, and preserving that time (also, let's do this for lunch too while we're at it). Make strategy a priority.

Back in the section on the beginner's mindset, I introduced the concept of thought partnership. One of the ways I help clients struggling to meet their 20% time is through one-on-one strategy sessions designed to help them maximize their time, sometimes helping to share the burden so that they only spend a few hours a month instead of one day a week on strategy. If you're constantly putting out fires and are unable to dedicate resources to planning and overall strategy, bring it up with your manager or your team. Perhaps there are internal or external resources already in place that could fulfill a thought partnership role for you, or a restructuring of responsibilities to accommodate this crucial strategy time.

7

Meetings, Redesigned with Empathy

You (yes, you) Can Fix Meetings

There's this amazing phenomenon about meetings and time: a meeting will take exactly the amount of time you allow for it. If you have an hour, it will take an hour. Somewhere along the way, the hour became the default for office meetings. But let's break down that hour: the first 10 minutes are waiting for the late people, who know you'll wait for them, and who will definitely drag your meeting out over the hour and keep their next meeting waiting. Yes, those people. The next 10–15 are bringing everyone up to speed who didn't read the email or weren't at the last meeting. Next, everyone important makes sure they get to talk. And then as the clock ticks down, the last 5–7 minutes ignites a pressure in the room and there's a rush for consensus, next steps, crossing agenda items off. What if you could skip that first 30 minutes, just by setting expectations in advance?

Friends, I'm not telling you change will happen overnight. But I am telling you that it will happen. You may not see yourself in a leadership role, but if you are planning meetings you are in a position of great power. You have the opportunity to show how different things can be, with a very validatable ROI to back it up.

You can design meetings that people want to be invited to that actually accomplish goals. Great meetings aren't made, they're *designed.*

Meetings Aren't for Planning—They're for Doing.

What was the last meeting you attended about? (Can you even remember?) And what was accomplished in that meeting? Most likely, if it was a really productive meeting, attendees left with assignments, maybe a decision was made, and you ended with a plan to reconvene. You had 4–9 (assuming here) people in a room for (assuming again here) an hour (or more!). That entire hour, the meter was running.

Your 4–9 attendees were all paid to be there. Think of the salaries or wages of those included. Add up the dollar value of the individuals' time spent in that room accomplishing next to nothing and you'll have a solid understanding of how meetings cost almost $541 billion in 2019.[15]

Start doing the work while you are all gathered together. Make decisions. Outline the project. You're not dragging people through their individual tasks, you're removing the need for many minor individual tasks (that, let's face it, probably wouldn't have been done

---

15 *The State of Meetings 2019.* Doodle. "The projected cost of pointless meetings in 2019." https://meeting-report.com/. Accessed February 2019.

by the next meeting anyway). Recognize and harness the collective brainpower in attendance and respect the incredible opportunity you have before you. Stop thinking of meetings as a forum to explore and start thinking of them as a collaboration session. Stop planning and start doing.

You must set a purpose for your meeting, which you'll include on your calendar invite. Most invites I see are something like "budget" or "planning." Those are vague and don't really mean anything—in fact, they could mean anything, so your meeting could drag on and on without an end. Your purpose should be specific, and not a secret. By reading the purpose, an attendee should be able to judge whether or not their attendance is valuable.

A good meeting purpose for "budget" would be "Present purchase plans and obtain approval from stakeholders"—JUST KIDDING! That would be an email. You'd send the purchase plans and request email approval with a deadline. See how easy this can be? For a real meeting with purpose, instead of "2020 vision" you would say "discuss opportunities for product line growth in 2020." You set the stage for an open-ended (yet, ideally, facilitated) conversation with "discuss" and gives a preview of the topic so people can prepare with "product line growth."

People tend to either under- or overshoot in goal setting for meetings. Don't get too ambitious and think you're going to plan an entire sales quarter or conference in one meeting. Conversely, don't go easy on your team and think "have discussion" is an acceptable goal. Make your goals actionable, achievable, realistic and impactful. At a maximum, set 2 goals per meeting (1 is perfectly acceptable). An example of good goals are "achieve consensus on event budget amount" or "delegate roles for spring festival," or my favorite: "identify roadblocks to see why project is stalled." Goals keep your meeting on track, ensuring you end the meeting with what you need to keep going. Now that you have all of the details nailed down, it's time to start the meeting planning.

Liminal Space: Let's Get Uncomfortable.

Comfort is the enemy of creation. Complacency prevents innovation. It's the reason why necessity is the mother of invention and why civilization's greatest minds questioned everything. Are you too comfortable? Is your team? Let's make them uncomfortable by creating liminal space.

The concept of liminal space is the idea that, by creating a psychologically uncomfortable (read: different) setting, the brain functions in a heightened state of awareness. It is like survival mode but instead of a perceived threat, there is a sense of things being not quite right, and a more urgent need to find solutions—even crazy ones.

This is one of the reasons Escape Rooms are so popular. It is a space created to introduce just enough discomfort and anxiety (there's that pesky timer, the locked door and the sense of competition) that you focus your mental resources collectively trying to find creative solutions.

There are plenty of different interpretations of liminal space (and some pretty weird new age beliefs about it that we won't get into here) but to me it makes more sense to describe the feeling instead of give you a definition.

You have experienced liminal space before: an airport before it's open, a school after closing or during the summer, a familiar store with the lights off, or even something as common as hallway, a stairwell or an elevator. It's the reception hall after the wedding is over and the lights come on to start cleaning up—a once crowded and alive space is now empty.

Liminal space is both the space between (the transitional space) and a different experience of a familiar space. How spooky is the mall after closing? It doesn't feel right without people in there and the lighting is strange. You are uncomfortable in a familiar place. Liminal space is not limited to physical spaces. Approximately half of your day comprises routine and habitual[16] behaviors—things you do exactly the same way, every single day, almost without thinking.

You are on autopilot. Do you ever drive home and realize you don't remember the journey? Most of us take the same way to work every day, shop at the same grocery store and even buy the same groceries every time.

That is plenty of space to get comfortable, predictable and settled. That pattern leaves no room for interpretation, innovation, or even a conscious registering of your actions.

There is a benefit to predictability and routine. Things are simplified. We know the Zuckerberg uniform works. In a 2014 interview, when asked why he wears the same thing every day (like a cartoon character), he replied "I really want to clear my life to make it so that I have to make as few decisions as possible about anything except how to best serve this community."

In the last few years we have seen the emergence of the capsule wardrobe, where women shed their overstuffed closets in

16 Neal, David T, Wood, Wendy and Wu, Mengiu (2014). The Pull of the Past: When Do Habits Persist Despite Conflict With Motives? *Personality and Social Psychology Bulletin*. Volume 37, Issue 11, pages 1428-1437.

favor of a sturdy ~20 piece interchangeable wardrobe. Minimalism is chic, abundance is out and Marie Kondo's *The Japanese Art of Tidying Up* is in over 4 million optimistically and partially decluttered homes (including mine).

Comfort in routine, predictability and simplicity create a safe place where—by eliminating decisions and even opportunity for risk—our minds stop processing our environment and slip into autopilot. We are not questioning, we are not challenged, and we surely aren't innovating.

I'm not suggesting that we throw your entire team into an abandoned shopping mall. But it is possible to tweak our experience and perception just enough to get us thinking creatively.

Liminal space can be created manually by deviating from a well-worn rut. We can take a new way home from work, we can try a new coffee spot, wear new patterns and try new groceries.

Ever get that tingly excited feeling when trying a new experience? That is the thrill of adrenaline from overcoming and benefiting from being in liminal space. It's like landing after your first skydive. You effing did it.

Liminal space is difficult to create in a professional environment, and discomfort is not something you want your employees to experience, but it can be done on a very simple level that still shakes things up and makes people feel slightly out of their element. Just enough to get the brain activity firing up, to create a feeling of having overcome the discomfort with a new experience.

One of the first things I like to do in a room full of bored-looking people is to make them switch seats. They look at me like I am insane. Some won't even participate. I call them out on it. I want them to be very uncomfortable. I might enjoy that a little bit. If I am facilitating a workshop in which I enter the room and the participants have already been occupying the space for another presentation, I make everyone stand up and sit somewhere different. It's not a power play or a control move. It's to a) get the blood flowing, b) get people to think a little differently, and c) create a clear division between *then* and *right now*. It's a physical reset that creates a mental reset, and it is very effective.

This is also a great technique if you start to see your audience losing focus. Even the most dynamic and captivating speakers give the audience space to let the mind wander. It's not their fault. It's human nature. We weren't meant to sit in chairs all day and we were never meant to stare at screens or listen to the same guy rattling off a thousand facts to us in a dimly lit and obnoxiously opulent hotel ballroom (remember that employee orientation from Chapter 1?). We are meant for action—chasing mammoths with spears and skinning our own rabbits, solving our own problems like our lives depended on it (because they did). We weren't designed for squinting at spreadsheets and struggling to reload staplers (seriously, why is that so hard?).

Moving rooms around, moving people around, changing lighting and changing the way information is presented are a few quick wins for justifying the use of liminal space. Maybe try an excursion to a new place for a brainstorm session or an activity that's out of the ordinary. Just try a slight adjustment and see how your creativity changes. Push your team a little further out of their comfort zone (in a pleasant yet freshly uncomfortable way) to see how they react.

Instead of booking a ballroom at a hotel, have your offsite

meeting in a non-traditional room. It doesn't matter if it's here or in Hawaii, a corporate conference room is still a corporate conference room. The elements are all familiar—pitchers of water, those weird leather writing pads, the gold-tipped pens you twist to open that come in only blue or black, the dusty projector and maybe a white board, if you're lucky. If not that, then a flipchart.

It's the same space, just a different building. And you wonder why the ideas are as stale as the wallpaper.

Think of what would happen if you gathered everyone for the planning meeting at a coworking space downtown. Or a classroom. Or a Chinese restaurant. Or an AirBnB in a NYC loft. If you want to leave dated, corporate thinking behind, you'll need to hide from it in a place it would never think to look.

Can't change the location? That's OK, you can still change the mood. I've ripped the skirts off of many a hotel conference table and rearranged the same U-shaped table configuration at least fifty times. Here is my quick checklist to instantly improve a boring meeting space:

1. **Remove as much of the corporate clutter as possible.** Ditch the pads, standard issue pens, writing palettes, water pitchers and tablecloths if you can.
2. **Replace it with surprising and thoughtful details.** Fun writing implements, stress balls, fidget spinners, candy bowls, brainstorming supplies—pick anything that contrasts the formal familiar room your meeting-goers expect.
3. **Level up your snack game.**

4. **Change the shape or layout of the space.**

5. **Add a mood-setting playlist.**

6. **Think of other ways to change expectations to change the tone.** Whether you greet meeting-goers as they enter with a warm cookie or a stack of Post-it Notes and a sharpie, or create a crepe paper tunnel to walk through, you can make the blandest of meeting spaces feel different.

For something slightly uncomfortable but not too far out of the familiar, you could try to ditch traditional nametags. I've done a few different takes on this—once, I had people write 1–3 words that allude to an interesting story about themselves, instead of their names. Mine was "82 Skydives." Others in the room were "cooked for Clinton," "auctioneer," and "escaped serial killer" (grammar is important on that one). This is a great opportunity to turn something expected (nametags) into something unexpected (genuine conversation, potential for empathy and icebreaker all in one).

You could potentially incorporate a theme. I once hosted a meeting with internal stakeholders whose buy-in I needed to purchase a $25,000 corporate license to Livestream. This team of leaders was constantly pitched to for purchases and was constantly in meetings. To set mine apart, I created a movie night. Instead of a conference room, I used a meeting room that had theatre seating and a big screen. I played a loop of silent movies and a jazzy retro soundtrack to make it feel special. The result was a completely different vibe, a much more easy-going tone and lively conversation that allowed us to make our sales pitch a lot more naturally as part of the conversation flow, versus a 1-on-20 presentation. Total budget: about $30.

I've also seen a lot of meeting facilitators skipping the slide deck in favor of a hand-illustrated flip chart with positive results.

QUESTIONS TO ASK YOURSELF:

1. **Do you really need a presentation and slides?**

   Do you have a lot of numbers or data to communicate? Could it be a handout instead? Can you speak in a compelling way where the deck isn't needed? Can you use posters or a flipchart instead to summarize key points? I'm sure you can find a more compelling way to deliver this information. Would you want to sit through your own presentation? If the slides are to aid in notetaking, consider providing a printed summary instead. If you need slides, keep the text to a minimum (think of TED Talk slides). Remember that people will read each slide, and it's impossible to read and listen at the same time.

2. **Where should the chairs go?**

   Chair placement sets the tone for your meeting. People should have sufficient space to feel comfortable, and the direction of the chairs dictates what kind of meeting it will be. Do you want a group of individuals all facing one presenter, or do you want to encourage collaboration and participation in a round? Seated, people will ideally have room to cross and uncross legs and arms without bumping a neighbor. Do you want one larger group or multiple smaller groups? Could you break groups into clusters around multiple tables?

3. **What's your technology policy?**

   Following the example of social events, it's perfectly acceptable to ask your guests to leave their laptops out of the meeting. No one likes a sly attendee pretending they're not emailing during the meeting. Sorry, my dears, no multitasking! Full participation, or don't show up.

4. **Do you need tables?**

   Do you have any activities that require them to write or type on a laptop? Will they have a lot of stuff with them? Will they be eating or drinking? If so, you'll want tables. You may be able to get by with side or end tables for drinks.

5. **Do you need chairs?**

   Probably, yes, but think about your meeting and consider the energy you can harness from a standing collaborative activity. Depending on the length of the meeting, you may not require an audience of chairs—though for accessibility it is important to have a few places for people to sit if they become tired (and if your meeting is longer than 20 minutes you may want a seated portion). Sometimes stools and high-top tables for leaning are good to have if you don't need formal tables and chairs.

6. **Does it really need to be private?**

   Regardless of your industry, I'm convinced that 99% of what you are saying is non-proprietary (I'm also convinced that 100% of what you say is ignored by anyone who may overhear). If you can remove the shroud of secrecy and privilege from your meeting, you'll open up more options for location.

7. **Do you really need a whiteboard? Or a flipchart?**

   The Design Sprint community may have me hanged for this one, but sometimes gathering and capturing ideas can be done in a different way. Maybe this meeting is just a facilitated discussion with one note-taker. Or maybe your whiteboard could be replaced with a roll of craft paper? I've done this many times to make a conference room feel different, and Post-it Notes stick to it like a dream. Line the walls with the stuff and use colorful markers to label different sections for different activities. I don't care how old you are, writing on the wall always feels a little bit mischievous.

8. **Does it need to be local?**

   Maybe there is somewhere a bit further out that could create some nice distance between your team and the office, letting minds clear and wander on the way to and from.

   With these considerations, you may realize what you thought were meeting must-haves were really just traditions. Try going without them. It may feel uncomfortable at first, but isn't that the point?

8

How Empathetic Research
Guides Problem-Solving

Again with the surveys

Imagine you are working on a project to help the homeless in your hometown. You hand out surveys to people you find on the street (or distribute them at a shelter). You ask multiple choice questions including:

Where do you sleep at night?

Are you a Veteran?

What is your gender?

How old are you?

Select your highest level of education completed.

Do you have a cell phone?

You receive a great demographic image of what the homeless population looks like and you set out on your project, armed with statistics and data to support your decisions. But what do you actually know about the experience of being homeless? What do you actually know about your user? What does their age, gender or educational background have to do with their needs? Or interests?

I selected the homeless for this example because I have no idea what it is like to be homeless. I have slept indoors every night of my entire life (definitely would never go camping) and I have been warm, cool, dry and fed every single night of my life. I have led a charmed life.

Because of this limited perspective, I do not understand the chain of events that could result in homelessness. I do not know how one becomes homeless. And I do not understand what it feels like. Even if I sleep on the street to simulate the experience, I still have a home to go back to and enough money to buy food, so I will never fully understand.

Your data is incomplete, and your experiment is inherently flawed. Did it occur to you that your printed survey, written in English, meant you created a selection bias to those that are literate in English, or had healthy vision? And how about your distribution: your sample size is exclusive to those who are homeless and choose to visit a shelter.

Your limited data can cause you to draw conclusions that may not be validated in a more in-depth study (for example, female veterans with a high school diploma are less likely to have a cell phone). I see this same logical fallacy[17] play out in many different

---

17 Specifically, my husband tells me in his edit of this section, the McNamara Fallacy or Simpson's Paradox.[18]
18 Did I ever tell you how we met? He was editing my work and I tracked him down in person to dispute his deletion of a comma I felt strongly about including.[19]
19 I dare you to find a better writer meet-cute.[20]

situations. Surveys are not the complete picture, and this data cannot and should not stand alone. Many fail-to-launch projects can be attributed to some version of this research misstep. Data has been collected, but it's not the right data.

The data you need—from which all development and creation should always begin—is empathetic data. And the only way to obtain empathetic data is to conduct empathetic research.

How to Gather Empathetic Data

Even with open-ended questions on an anonymous survey, you still aren't getting the valuable empathetic data that comes from studying your customer and stepping inside their experience. The only way to fully understand them is to empathize with them, and this is done through research.

Empathetic research is similar to ethnographic research in that both are done while studying and observing people.

As Jane Goodall experienced with the chimpanzees of Tanzania, mere observation is not enough. She lived among them, participated in their culture and forged a profound understanding for them. I would say that Ms. Goodall has significant empathy for chimpanzees.

There was a great family-friendly reality show a while back called *Undercover Boss*. The CEO or other high-ranking official of a well-known company would put on a disguise, travel to a franchise of his own company and work the lowest paying job for a week. Nearly every episode resulted in the CEO crying or near-crying while viewers at home witnessed the precise gut-punch moment of empathy. The

---

20 You should know that, ultimately, the comma did not survive.

CEOs were usually so moved by their experience and by the stories of the people they worked beside during the experiment that at the end (spoiler alert!) they would give the employee a paid vacation, or college tuition or a promotion.

It is not always necessary (or advisable) to live among those you are studying, and there are many other ways to conduct an empathy study. I do not expect you to give up your life to live among your user. That level of commitment, while powerful, is unnecessary. There is no need to fully inhabit your user when you have a user as a resource. You need not become the user to empathize with them.

What you must do, however, is seek to understand their experience and to get to the root of their experience, using their own words and actions as context. By making an experience that seems foreign more relatable, empathy comes naturally. Shifting your perspective on an alternate experience to make it feel more about you, or someone close to you, will make you more empathetic. But not every experience is relatable. So how do you find empathy?

By looking for a connection. A spark of familiarity. Commonalities are everywhere, and even someone whose daily experience seems completely foreign to you has something in common with you.

You may work in an office and your study participants may work on a factory line, or maybe you lead a team of designers and you need to understand a team of developers. There are similarities in your experience, and finding them is the key to the application of empathy in the context of business development and strategy. Maybe you can't find that connection. Can you take John Steinbeck's advice and imagine someone you know? Can you put a friend or family member in the shoes of your study subject?

Sometimes that twinge of recognition isn't immediately obvious. Creating a user persona will help to humanize your users and help you to forge empathetic bonds with them as you seek to create valuable experiences for them. It will also be useful in trying to communicate and inspire this empathy in those on your team who are not present for research.

User personas are frequently used in marketing research to humanize the user, and ultimately garner empathy for them, though rarely is it identified as such. By naming and personifying the customer, they become an identifiable and knowable individual, helping to target the messaging and interact more authentically. Marketing messaging is directed to one person: Tara The Runner or Todd The Pet Store Owner, who shops online and hates paying for shipping (or some variation thereof).

A good persona goes beyond basic sales demographics and incorporates needs, desires, behaviors, goals, preferences, pain points and struggles. When marketing teams begin to develop a persona, they conduct (or purchase) large amounts of market research and demographic information. As we've learned so far in this book, that data is not sufficient.

In order to understand what your customer needs in terms of their product use and consumption, you must understand the need that prompts the product development in the first place. To understand their needs, you must empathize with them. The only way to find this data is through empathetic research, and so to build a solid and reliable user persona you must conduct an empathy study.

And while experiences broadcast on TV are far more dramatic

than real life, imagine what would happen if your CEO (or you) anonymously worked the lowest paying job at your company for a week. What would happen if all of your product engineers had to take customer service calls for a day? Would the power of that experience change anything? If so, it might be time for an empathy study.

When to Use Empathy Research

As I've experienced it, the purpose for empathetic research falls into two main categories:

Empathy to Guide a Project (a project that hasn't yet launched)

or

Empathy for Problem Solving (a project that has already launched)

The first folds neatly into your project ideation and development phases, and I'll show you how that works in a bit. The second is when you're trying to bail out a failing project, or it's not going the way you anticipated, or you're not really sure what the problem is. Things don't need to be dire to introduce empathy research, but when all hope is lost it's not a waste of time, either. You may want to consider using empathy research for problem solving in scenarios similar to these:

Scenario A: A project with so much time and money invested has all the makings of a success—the spreadsheets check out, the numbers look good, and based on historical data, everything should work. And yet, upon launch, the project falls flat.

Scenario B: Using existing data and customer demographics, a company knows exactly who their customer is and what they want. Yet the marketing targeted directly to this customer archetype fails to increase sales or attract new customers.

Scenario C: Taking into account multiple customer complaints about a service, the team launches a new solution to that service that should eliminate the complaints. However, the customers do not take advantage of the solution and it creates more complaints.

There are hundreds of other situations that could benefit from an empathy study but let these examples guide your thinking to understand that a lack of empathy may be the reason for these failures. Things can be turned around! Your project isn't dead.

The most resistance I've received in suggesting empathy research has been around the time commitment, but, really, you can dedicate a few days to this. The payoff is worth it. I promise. Also around secrecy. Is what you're doing truly that proprietary? Is it worth keeping it under wraps if the launch is blind and you have no idea what your user will really think?

I know as a large company you are used to multiple NDAs and talking generically about your super-top-secret projects. And traditional sales and marketing rules have you trained to heavily promote and create anticipation for a grand debut, launching a perfect product from the start. Apple Keynote goals aside, are you really creating additional value or guaranteeing a solid launch by doing those things?

I'll reiterate two points already made in this book.

1. **If nothing ever changes, then nothing ever changes.**

    If what you're doing is working flawlessly, why are you
    wasting your time reading my book? You should be enjoying
    the fruits of your labor on a beach somewhere with a drink
    served in a coconut. This is not a very good beach read. Maybe
    try something by Sophie Kinsella?

    If, on the other hand, you find yourself open to other
    options to solve your seemingly unsolvable problems (and
    you're not on the beach) then you are opening yourself and
    your organization up to the possibility of change. Real change.
    The kind that gets featured in *Fast Company* and *Inc*. You
    don't get articles written about you for playing it safe.

2. **If you want people to support, champion and genuinely
    participate in your projects, you need to bring them into
    the fold early.**

    You're creating a unique bond between producer and consumer
    that allows for more free-flowing and candid feedback; creates
    opportunities to pivot early, validate and adjust; and build a
    user group ready to rally around your project.

    Involve the users you want to create for. They will
    be more impressed and involved if you demonstrate genuine
    interest in them than they would be with an over-hyped grand
    launch.

Moving Forward with Empathetic Research

When I began running Design Sprints (remember those?) after

reading the how-to on the Google Ventures blog, I was first introduced to user research. User research in this form most closely resembles usability studies, which now makes up a large portion of my work for clients. Usability studies are for testing a user's interaction with a prototype or existing product in order to gather feedback to implement into future iterations. For digital products, click tracking and mouse path (cursor) tracking are often combined with biometric data (retina tracking, pulse tracking, video) to understand a user's engagement with a product. This is followed by an interview to learn what they like and do not like about the prototype and identify what changes should be made. During a Design Sprint, the prototypes are not necessarily digital so the tests are much less sophisticated. In the user interviews of those early Sprints, I found myself digging deeper than the other test administrators and craving more and more insight into the user's experience. It took years to understand that what I was doing was empathy research, that it could provide unparalleled data and insight for the development of products and services, and that it was a vital and absent component in almost every project I'd seen. I made it a mission to spread this knowledge to everyone I could, to emphasize the importance of including empathy research before building *anything* and to prove a demonstrable value to skeptical decision makers. Then to make it accessible to all.

9

How to Conduct Empathetic Research

This is the terribly short but extremely accessible guide to the research methods necessary to run your own empathy study. They are resource-light, scalable and valuable, and empathy is the key to nearly any solution. I really can't think of any reason why you wouldn't want to conduct an empathy study.

An empathy study can be added into any project timeline (even after the fact, as troubleshooting) and your goals can fall within any of these areas:

• **Identify a problem and a market need.** Instead of reverse-engineering product-market fit, beginning with research can uncover a problem that needs solving, the one that your product (or service, or program) solves.

• **Understand the needs of a customer.** Empathetic interviewing can provide insight into what a customer needs (and how best to solve their problem).

• **Find the right focus for a phase 1 product.** Knowing where to start is one of the greatest paralytics of large projects. Through research you can identify the best entry point to focus development efforts on for early launch.

• **Design a more custom-feeling product.** The more you understand your customer, the more you can tailor the experience directly to their needs, making your product feel bespoke (even at scale).

• **Determine the best time and method for a launch.** Knowing your customer's habits and communication style—which is completely obtainable through this research—can guide marketing efforts, promotional strategies and delivery methods.

• **Determine where and how to sell the product.** In-depth customer data will help you understand how best to reach them, and how to accommodate their buying habits.

• **Validate or invalidate assumptions.** A mistake many companies make is treating assumptions as facts. What you believe to be true (that is, anything unsubstantiated by complete customer data—again, not just a survey) is an assumption until it is validated. That means your assumption is actually a testable hypothesis. Assumptions can be tested and validated quite easily and without much time or money, but they also can save you from making very expensive decisions, which is why they are such a crucial investment.

• **Uncover alternate uses and opportunities for a product.** Through testing and validation, you'll know how your user engages with your product and find potential secondary users or uses for the product.

• **Beta test incomplete ideas or concepts.** This is more validation that can be achieved through the type of research you're about to learn. When a product is released into the consumer marketplace fully polished and complete but the launch is unsuccessful, it is very expensive to figure out why. With lower-resolution prototypes, beta launches, conceptual testing and research, it's possible to avoid costly missteps and be somewhat assured of a successful launch, armed with the data to back it up.

Step One: Define Your User

Whose feedback would be the most valuable? For whom do you need to experience empathy? Whose problem are you trying to understand and solve?

You may find that your solution has a secondary and even tertiary user. This may not be immediately obvious so remain open to the possibility that others might be affected by or interested in your solution as you create it. You can always pause to gather their insights as well throughout the development process.

Step Two: Research the Problem

To solve the problem, you must first understand the problem and make sure you are solving the right problem. Remember problem framing? Do that now.

Step Three: Research the People Experiencing the Problem

You may find that researching the people's experience informs the problem framing, and after the empathetic research you may need to return to problem framing. That, as we have learned so far in this book, is not a failure[21]. It's an iteration, a pivot, new information—whatever it is, it's supported by data and thus extremely useful and meaningful to your project.

Here is where the methods split into different processes. There are three main approaches to researching a person's experience. They are:

Immersion: Think Jane Goodall and *Undercover Boss*. This is living among your test group and fully participating in their experience.

Observation: Watching but not interacting with your test group. This is scientific field research, and while legal permission should be obtained, your subjects should not be aware of your presence.

Interview: In my opinion, the most powerful research tool is the user themselves. Interviews should be conducted adhering to specific guidelines but will yield the most valuable information.

Many projects will combine all or some of each method and the data mined from each experience will vary greatly, yet most likely support other data gathered. We'll dive into each method deeper with clear steps for execution, but in the beginning each study starts with the same steps.

Using the Immersion Method

You must decide to what degree you will embed with your subjects, and maintain ethical and legal standards. They key to successful immersion is in an authentic experience. For example, you can't really research the economy coach experience while flying in First Class (nor the other way around). It's also important to blend in and participate fully but not be treated as a researcher. You don't want a filtered experience and you don't want a performance.

The CEO of a prominent southern US-based cloud computing company spends time sitting in the customer call center with service representatives quite frequently, fielding calls himself to understand the problems his customers are experiencing. He could easily rely on reports, stats, data and second- or third-hand information delivered to him by other employees—information that would probably be passed up 2–4 levels before it ever reached him. Instead, he wants first-hand experience with the customers calling for help and the representatives helping them. In one video about this experience, he laughs as he realizes he doesn't know how to solve one of the problems presented to him in a call. "Let me bring in the expert," he says, gesturing for the representative seated next to him to jump in. This is immersion. It doesn't always require six years among the chimpanzees.

To become immersed and to ensure the most authentic experience, upfront planning is required. Here is how immersion should be planned:

1. **Set a goal for research.** You'll need to have a general idea of what experience you'll be immersing in (in the latest example, it was the experience of helping a customer solve a problem). It may be a similarly narrowed focus. It may also be an information-gathering immersion or something more broad, especially in the case that the exact problem to solve has yet to

be identified. Either way, a goal for the immersion will need to be set.

2. **Set a schedule.** Will you be there a few hours? A few days? A few weeks? How long do you think you will need to understand the problem and the way a user experiences it? At a minimum, I would recommend a half-day. A few full days, if you are able. From experience, I have found that anyone is able to be on their best behavior and that the natural façade we all put forth when entertaining company will last for about 2 days. After that, even the most earnest of hosts begins to let the frayed edges show and you'll get the *real* experience.

3. **Have a host or liaison.** Enlist the help of a user or customer, or someone already well-embedded into your selected audience (or perhaps one of your evangelists?). While they will not speak for all of your users, they will act as your host and tour guide throughout your research. This can be more than one person. They'll be extremely useful in cluing you in to any cultural differences, social expectations, or other minor insider details like where to park or what to wear or even how to get into the building.

4. **Create a list of questions to guide your research and notetaking.** Know what it is you need to know.

During immersion research, you'll want to do a pulse check every so often. A pulse check is a brief biological and psychological checkpoint to help stay focused and aware of your experience. Take special note of how you feel. What struggles you have. What joys you experience. Watch how others around you react—is your reaction different? What is it really like to be where you are and do what you are doing? What new questions do you have? What have you learned so far? What has surprised you? A good rate for pulse checks is about 4 per day.

Using the Observation Method

Authenticity, anonymity and invisibility are the most important elements of observation. Here you must also adhere to legal and ethical standards

Just like with nature documentaries, you are just observing and not interfering. Do not stir the pot or create scenarios to help your observations along. Just witness. The observation method is a few degrees removed from the immersion method, while they share certain similarities. In observation, you will not be interacting with your subjects and should go largely unnoticed by them. You will not have the opportunity to interview or to ask questions (though it is possible to combine studies—we'll cover that later).

With observational research, your notes should remain as impartial and as direct as possible. Do not draw conclusions. Write exactly what you see and how you see it. You can write questions within your observations but do not make assumptions. Example: You are observing passengers at a bus terminal. Your note may be *17 people buy hot dogs before getting on the bus*, but you shouldn't include conclusions like *because they are hungry; because it is lunch time; because the bus ride is long*. Even if you know those things are most likely true.

When planning observational research, you'll need:

1. **A goal for your research,** just as with the Immersion method.

2. **Clearance or permission to observe.** Remember that people must be informed if they are being recorded and must sign consent forms for most unique instances in which that footage will be used—unless they are in a public place in the United States (even then, it's a respectful gesture). However, you may need permission to observe within the space. Research what is legal where you are conducting your study.

3. **A schedule for research.** For observation, 1–4 hours is usually sufficient, though more is always helpful if you can swing it.

Using the Interview Method

Empathetic interviewing is a delicate balancing act. You want to ask the right questions and document the right data, but in order to get the most authentic and valuable information from your subject, you have to make the process feel informal, non-intimidating, transparent and important all at the same time. It's challenging, and you only get one shot to do it right (you can't go back and re-interview the same people in a different way to course-correct, though you can usually access their perspective again in the testing phase). Here's how you can prepare for interviewing in advance:

1. **Define a goal for research.** This is a pretty standard step in research planning, as you've noticed so far.

2. **Let your interviewees know what's coming.** There's no reason for secrecy. If people know what you are trying to accomplish, they may be more inclined to help. This can be as simple as a quick email to those who might be interviewed outlining the purpose of the research.

3. **Identify a research liaison.** Like the hosts for immersion research, your evangelists or contacts will be extremely useful, especially in helping you contextualize your research emapthetically—how does your showing up for interviewing fit in to your subjects' experience? Is there anything going on recently that might impact your interviews? I learned this lesson with a very big research mistake. I once conducted a series of empathetic interviews with third shift manufacturing workers (those from 7pm to 7am). I showed up at 4am with a human resources representative and a clipboard and started pulling people into a closed-blinds meeting room. That first day of interviewing, my participants were shaking, nervous and generally non-communicative. The feedback they were giving me was overwhelmingly positive, to the point that it didn't seem believable. What I didn't know was that just two weeks earlier, a pretty big merger had occurred. People were afraid of losing their jobs, and here I was making it seem like they

were interviewing for them. No wonder I wasn't getting honest answers. Now, I always ask what's going on.

Remember your evangelists? When building an internal product, your evangelists are those brought into the fold early to help obtain the buy-in of their larger teams. Educate these evangelists on your goals and your plan to achieve them. Count on them to spread the word and bring their teams on board, hopefully ensuring greater participation in your empathy interviews and research.

With evangelists, your interviews are two-fold. You are interviewing your evangelists on one set of questions and information, trying to find out how best to interview their teams while also gathering information on their experience. You can also ask them about the daily experience of their teams, but note that this is not a substitute for interviewing their teams.

If your product is external or for customers, you won't have the benefit of evangelists convincing customers to participate, and you may want to offer an incentive for their time and feedback. Traditional ethics states that if they receive anything in exchange for their feedback, the results are invalidated. Giving them a free lunch or discount (jab and a jab, remember?) potentially sways their opinion when you interview them. However, common sense says a little courtesy for their time can help ensure that they will actually participate in your study. I find a $20 Amazon gift card is easy to distribute and is always appreciated when appropriate.

To make an interviewee feel the most at ease, they should be interviewed in a familiar space. On their own territory yields the best results (e.g., going to their home, office or workspace instead of bringing them to a common place). By all counts, avoid spaces associated with disciplinary or negative consequences (e.g., the principal's office, HR, or, in my tragic example of the manufacturing workers, the room where a layoff might happen). Neutral territory is a good second choice—somewhere neither party has any experience or association with. This also helps create liminal space (see, we're tying it all together so nicely here at the end!).

You want to bring in transparency right at the beginning and let your interviewee know why you need their feedback and how much of an impact it will have. This is beyond a "we value your feedback" type of exchange and requires authentic honesty. "We are asking for your help because we want to design an app people will actually use, and your feedback helps us create that experience." That's a much more human approach, and one that establishes a little bit of two-way empathy. Your interviewee sees that you have goals, they understand your needs, and now you can get to understanding theirs.

After you've leveled with your interviewee and established transparency, you should make them comfortable. Don't just jump in and start asking what will feel like a numbered list of direct questions, so that they feel they are on trial. Imagine that you have just been introduced to them. Get to know them in a slightly less structured way. How do you talk to people at networking events? How do you get to know friends of friends? Build a rapport with your interviewee so that they relax.

You can do this by explaining your role in the project and providing a little background personal information. Humanize yourself. Use this to ask them about their role by comparison. As you are gathering this empathetic data, try to give the conversations a more organic feel as opposed to a formalized interview that might feel more like a performance review. It's a conversation, not a Q&A.

To help keep the conversation flowing, the interviewer should not be the notetaker, but no more than 2–3 people should be present.

Notes should include quotes and statements as well as observations (body language and other non-verbal indications). Your notes should also avoid interpretation; instead, write down exactly what you see and hear instead of trying to explain what you think the person means.

Recording interviews is tricky, especially if the interviewees are employees. Be sure to obtain consent for any recordings, audio or video, prior to the interview, and be aware that knowledge of being recorded will skew some feedback in addition to making it more difficult to make your interviewee comfortable.

Your questions should start out broad and become more narrowed toward the end. Initially, you want to create opportunities for open-ended longform responses. Allow the interviewee opportunities to tell a story (or several). Not only will they open up as they begin recounting their story, but you will receive a much more complete idea of their experience than you would from a one or two word (or yes or no) answer. Structure your questions so that they require longer answers.

You also need to realize and harness the power of silence. People are uncomfortable in silence and will usually fill the space by talking more than necessary. Interviewers tend to begin a question as soon as the interviewee stops talking. Wait for that dead air and see if there is more to the answer. Balance this with being mindful of long, awkward pauses but give plenty of breathing room around your questions. Try to avoid suggesting answers or completing their sentences as well to keep their answers more pure.

Try not to infer or direct with your questions, but keep them neutral. For example, rather than ask "Why do you like this product?" you should ask "how do you feel about this product?" You should also leave out information that could indicate how others respond to the same questions (example, "Most people seem to think..." or "Usually...").

You also shouldn't limit your questions to a singular topic such as your product or related experience. Instead, try to understand broadly other experiences that might influence perceptions or interactions with your product. Remember that you want a complete picture and not just a sketch of your user.

You'll finish by asking for more clarification, revisiting things the interviewee has said and digging a little deeper with specific phrasing. This will balance out the more open-ended beginning and help close out the interview.

The main questions set should be determined and worked through with your group prior to conducting the interviews, while others may arise in the moment and be interview-specific. Don't be afraid to deviate from the script if it makes sense, but be sure to capture similar information sets from each person interviewed.

Synthesizing Empathetic Research

The empathetic data you've collected through your research may seem too scattered to share, because you are used to hard numbers and facts. I challenge you to find new metrics in your data by spotting trends (which you'll begin to do naturally during your interviews) and finding ways to communicate what has been learned.

No doubt there were words that came up with again and again, or feelings expressed that were common. Present these findings to your group (maintaining anonymity, of course) by sharing statements like "of 30 people interviewed, 19 felt they were struggling to keep up with production demands" and "only 2 people interviewed were not interested in learning new job skills."

Turn insights into stories to convey humanity and feeling in your report. Pull direct quotes and first-hand accounts directly from the interviews to help your team really experience empathy for the interviewees. Remember that your entire goal is to humanize data so that the story is deeper than just numbers or a survey. Use these insights to stay on track and remember who you're creating for—and solve their problem the best you can.

10

How to Get Buy-In to
Do New Things

Now What?

You now have in your toolkit some of the most powerful and competitive skills in experience design and product development, and (while you're not quite qualified for a User Experience Design job) you're ready to start building faster, testable and empathy backed projects internally and externally that solve problems. The importance of making good experiences accessible cannot be emphasized enough, and while we are working to do better work, the opportunity for empathetically designed workplaces becomes more evident. I urge you to use these methods to improve things for those that work with you, even if you do not believe yourself to be in a position of power.

Leadership Buy-In for the Work You Want to Do

To make your small changes have a ripple effect throughout

your organization—and often, to access resources you may need to do things the right way—leadership buy-in is a must-have. Even if you find yourself in a leadership role and have carte blanche to pursue any project and any new process you like, at some point you'll still need buy-in for your new ideas. And you'll want it, because beyond just permission to explore, good buy-in acts as an endorsement. Not all buy-in is an endorsement—and it rarely is synonymous with complete and full trust—but that's where validation comes in.

To access buy-in at stage 1, you'll need to think smaller. Asking for everything you want up front, or for your grand project in full, is a mistake. You'll need to work up to that. Think of the Grand Canyon, where a river carved through stone just because it stuck with it so long and kept going. Think of yourself as the river, chipping slowly away at the stone until you've created a chasm. It's not overnight, it's certainly not easy, and it probably won't feel like you've done much at all until you look back at how far you've come.

My philosophy on getting buy-in is this: Instead of asking one big question whose answer is no, ask a thousand tiny questions whose answers are all yes. Get buy-in for the smallest version of what you want to do, ask that smallest first questions whose answer is yes. Instead of trying to change your entire organization with one meeting (or manifesto about meetings, if you're anything like me), make one small improvement in the direction you'd like to change meetings. If you know you need people to want to participate in your later big project, and you want to make a clear delineation between "the way we've always done it" and your pioneering new creative way, design an experience that shows the differences. Use empathy for your participants to make the experience—even a 5 minute brainstorm experience—meaningful.

Designing with empathy for your users means that if leadership is your user (the person you need to sell to), they deserve a bit of empathy as well. For the most part, senior and executive leadership tends to fit a certain mold, regardless of what they look like, and they tend to have things in common. Things that most likely led them down a path of leadership. Not all will meet these criteria, but, for the most part, leaders are:

- Risk averse
- Slow to make decisions
- Afraid of looking dumb
- Not overly preoccupied by details or process
- A bit removed from the inner workings of the company

Most leaders became leaders by doing the exact same thing over and over again in the exact same way until they themselves got leadership buy-in to keep doing the same things over and over again in the exact same way. If your company has been around awhile, chances are that stability and consistency have kept them where they are. What's interesting about leadership is that they only tend to see what's working or a polished final product. They don't see the first 20 drafts, they see a rehearsed executive presentation. They typically are not informed of the details or process it takes to get there (which is why they often have critical feedback of a few small changes that require potentially months of re-development!).

Can you start bringing them into the fold on new processes

early? Can you show them an ROI on the benefit of shorter, smaller testable projects? Can you get buy-in by showing dollars and hours saved when a change request is made earlier in the process?

If you treat your leaders like your customers, you can learn what motivates them and find a way to bring it to them. You can research them much like you would a customer by spending time with them and asking questions. Ask them to lunch—bold move, but try it. At the very least, try to sit in on meetings and observe how they talk, what kinds of questions they ask. Try to find out what is important to them. Conduct an informal empathy study on them and use the data to win their buy-in.

As you learn what your leaders value, you can also start to understand their problems. If you understand their problems, you can find ways to prove how the work you do will solve those problems. While you're solving their problems, you'll be redefining the relationship. Think about how your relationship is now. Even in just having to ask for buy-in, the relationship feels somewhat adversarial. As you gain empathy for them, you're understanding their problems and finding out how you can solve them, and you're aligning with their goals. If you can make your work align with their goals, you'll have more buy-in than you ever need. By shifting from an adversarial to a collaborative relationship, you'll be working together in a really unique way and solving problems that benefit everyone.

How to Eat the Elephant

There are problems and challenges that seem insurmountable, especially when the odds (team size, budget, deadline, restrictions, limitations) are not in our favor. Every big unsolvable problem is just a tangled mess of tiny, solvable problems. I tend to focus so much on the big picture that the details overwhelm me and I start to spiral. My husband always pulls me out of the spiral with the same reminder, in question form:

How do you eat an elephant?

The answer, if you don't know, is one bite at a time. The idea of eating an entire whole elephant (which I'm pretty sure violates some laws but for the sake of this adorable metaphor just go with me on this) is overwhelming. It's enormous. That's like 12,000 pounds. There's no way I could fit that in my belly at one time.

But when you break it down into small bites, it's not so bad. Just remember not to look back at all the remaining bites and you'll probably be OK. In fact, you could eat a bite a day for years and probably get through it. Don't check my math on that.

There's the story of the Greek wrestler Milo, who lifted the same calf every day. While the calf got slowly heavier and eventually became a bull, Milo was able to lift the fully grown bull. You can't just lift the bull on day one. You have to work up to it. The same goes for problem-solving: you can't just solve your biggest problem in a 2-hour workshop.

What you can do is frame the problem and find all the tiny little micro-problems that tangle up to make this big web of a problem. Find all of the solvable problems and prioritize them. Map them. Find their interdependencies. Pull each wire out of the mess one by one, until you have a neat stack of wires.

To uncover the root of your problem and the smallest solvable part of it, you know that you can conduct empathetic research. You'll be armed with data to justify every decision you make for the rest of the project, and the voice of the user (for whom the entire solution is being developed) to guide you. Insights from your research help keep a project on track and the end goal a common one.

And instead of letting all of your success or failure hinge on one single finished product, you're reducing the pressure by creating a safe-to-fail zone where you can test small parts of your unfinished concept and know exactly how each next step should go. You've created an environment where failure has been redefined as validation, and where there are no bad ideas—just testable hypotheses. Your strategy and development cycle is innovative; not just because you've thrown more sticky notes at the problem but because your collaboration is more authentic, empathetic and productive. By leveraging the tools in this book, you have embraced a truly unique and empathetic competitive edge, and can go forth to scale your methods organization-wide, knowing that small changes are just a bite of an elephant, and with enough of them, you'll eat the whole thing.

Acknowledgements

For this book to even have made it to this point took so many coincidences that even I am surprised we are here. To all who have contributed, positively and negatively, to its creation, I thank you—each roadblock made it a better book; each voice of support affirmed I was on the right path.

With immense love and gratitude to my husband, Jim Publicover, for his sacrifices and strength the last three years. For everything you've personally done to help me succeed—from long stretches alone with twin infants while I travelled for work, to making me a perfect cup of coffee every single morning we've been together without fail (when you don't even drink coffee). For editing this book in between work and being a father and a husband and giving yourself fully to all three. I forgive every comma you've removed from my work for everything else you've added to my life. Nobody could have (or would have) done what you've done for me, and I'll be making it up to you the rest of my life.

To Genevieve Wicker, Aunt Vivi to my boys: You're a mama bear, a therapist, a moral compass, a tech support hotline and a sister. You can infuse levity into even the most difficult situation. Your capacity for love, kindness and generosity is saintly, and you inspire me to be better to others. Thank you for being the first to hug me when I finished my first draft.

To my mom (Beverly) and to Russ for the bottomless support and encouragement, for always pitching in with the kids and for making me feel worthy of my accomplishments. As promised, Mom, I didn't even write about you. Love you!

To my dad for always pushing me to figure it out on my own in order to learn a lesson: I did it!

To Alice Ballenger, whose thought partnership and strategic prowess showed me the true potential of my business and helped me put all the puzzle pieces together—an alignment that changed the complete trajectory of everything I thought I was doing (even though it meant rewriting this book for a third time).

To Leah Williams, publicist extraordinaire, who stepped in at the 11th hour and knew exactly what to do, and who extinguishes my self doubt with a single text. You're fantastic and I'm so lucky to have you.

To Kat & Justin Jackson of Wilder&, for creating the most perfect brand aesthetic for Tiny Piñata that's just the right balance between fun rebellion and serious business, and for always creating something better than I imagined—even from my vague and nonsensical descriptions. You're both amazing and patient. Seriously, thank you.

To Stephanie Hannus, for designing this gorgeous cover so perfectly and so Me, for helping me through the process when I thought all hope was lost—and for always picking up right where we left off.

To my weekly Lean Coffee crew and early readers: Ross Chapman, Maicol Parker-Chavez, David Holl and Douglas Struble. For over a year our transcontinental chats have been the collaboration this solo operation needs. You're the coworkers I never knew I always needed, and you make this business so much less lonely. I raise my Big Drank to you all.

To the clients who trust me with their pet projects, their dreams, their work babies and even sometimes their livelihoods—from the entirety of my heart and my soul, thank you. Your trust pulls me out of bed, energized and inspired, to join you in the trenches and help you get your work done. Without you, none of this exists.

And finally, to the companies + individuals in my working life who created environments no one could possibly thrive in—thanks for not making me comfortable and complacent. I might have stayed, and this book might never have happened.

Notes

CHAPTER ONE: AN INTRODUCTION TO EMPATHETIC DESIGN

1 Actual attempted solutions to this problem carried out by other organizations.
2 McCusker, Deb & Wolfman, Ilene (1998). Loyalty in the Eyes of Employers & Employees.Workforce.

3 Murali, Sachin & Poddar, Aayush & Seema, A. (2017). Employee Loyalty, Organizational Performance & Performance Evaluation – A Critical Survey. IOSR Journal of Business and Management (IOSR-JBM). 19. 00-00.

CHAPTER TWO: WHY EMPATHETIC DESIGN MATTERS

4 Provine, Robert R. "Yawning: The Yawn Is Primal, Unstoppable and Contagious, Revealing the Evolutionary and Neural Basis of Empathy and Unconscious Behavior." American Scientist, vol. 93, no. 6, 2005, pp. 532–539.

5 Rundle, Brian & R. Vaughn, Vanessa & Stanford, Matthew. (2015). Contagious yawning and psychopathy. Personality and Individual Differences. 33–37.

6 Steinbeck, John. The Grapes of Wrath. New York: Penguin Classics, 1992. Print.

7 Gross, Terry. "Fresh Air" Chris Rock On Finding The Line Between Funny And 'Too Far.' December 2014.

CHAPTER THREE: EMPATHY IN PRACTICE

8 In this book, please interpret "user" to mean your employee, customer, student, participant and any other person for whom you may be solving a problem or creating a solution.

9 Vlaskovits, Patrick. Henry Ford, Innovation, and That "Faster Horse" Quote. Harvard Business Review. August 29, 2011.

10 We're talking strategically developed surveys capturing scientific data sent to a wide and varied group, not your Google survey.

11 LaValle, Steve; Lesser, Eric; Shockley, Rebecca; Hopkins, Michael S; Kruschwitz, Nina.; Big Data, Analytics and the Path From Insights to Value, MIT Sloan Management Review, Cambridge Vol. 52, Iss. 2, (Winter 2011): 21-32.

12 In the early 2000s I met an IT helpdesk employee at Apple who told me that nobody could service Job's Mac because it had a crazy custom operating system. I have been unable to confirm this in my research which is disappointing, because I always thought it was a neat anecdote and have widely (WIDELY) spread it as fact.

13 Marra, Chris. Building for Emerging Markets: The Story Behind 2G Tuesdays. http://code.facebook.com. October 27, 2015.

14 We all know the story of Post-It Notes' accidental creation by a low-ranking 3M employee.

CHAPTER SEVEN: MEETINGS, REDESIGNED WITH EMPATHY

15 *The State of Meetings 2019.* Doodle. "The projected cost of pointless meetings in 2019." https://meeting-report.com/. Accessed February 2019.

16 Neal, David T, Wood, Wendy and Wu, Mengiu (2014). The Pull

of the Past: When Do Habits Persist Despite Conflict With Motives? Personality and Social Psychology Bulletin. Volume 37, Issue 11, pages 1428-1437.

CHAPTER EIGHT: HOW EMPATHETIC RESEARCH GUIDES PROBLEM-SOLVING

17 Specifically, my husband tells me in his edit of this section, the McNamara Fallacy or Simpson's Paradox.

18 Did I ever tell you how we met? He was editing my work and I tracked him down in person to dispute his deletion of a comma I felt strongly about including.

19 I dare you to find a better writer meet-cute.

20 You should know that, ultimately, the comma did not survive

CHAPTER NINE: HOW TO CONDUCT EMPATHETIC RESEARCH

21 Well, it is a failure, but one that is very much a goal of your newfound methodology and one that should be welcomed.

About the Author

Dana Publicover is the founder of Tiny Piñata, a consulting firm that strategizes and runs workshops with companies who have problems to solve, ideas to explore or changes to make. Her experience spans the industries of publishing, healthcare, media, advertising, textile, transportation, nonprofits and higher-level education. She has run empathetic research studies for diverse groups that include young asthmatics, homebound elderly patients, third shift manufacturing workers, police officers and first year teachers.

Her workshops and strategies have supported the design of mobile and web applications, medical devices, corporate culture, retail spaces, customer communications and marketing strategies.

Dana has worked with teams all over the US and in France, China, India and the UK. She has trained with Google, IDEO, Design Sprint Academy, Stanford d.School and AJ&Smart.

Outside of work, Dana is a true-crime-watching book-loving twin mom who believes Saturday night is best spent pair programming with her husband.

Resources

Many of the concepts and processes introduced in this book have corresponding resources available for free download on the Tiny Piñata website, including tools for meeting design and running user testing. These can be found at:

https://www.tinypinata.xyz/resources

Made in the USA
Monee, IL
21 January 2022

89580689R00080